Beginning iOS Development with Swift: Create Your Own iOS Apps Today

1st Edition

Contents

Introduction 6

Chapter 1 - Getting Started...8

Downloading Xcode From The Apple Developer Website 8

Downloading Xcode From The Mac App Store 9

Overview of Xcode 10

Chapter 2 - Outlets and Actions (I) 11

A Simple Alert App 11

Adding some Swift code 21

Connecting our Button to Code 23

Chapter 3 - Outlets and Actions (II) 26

A Simple Calculator App 26

Adding Outlets 28

Connecting the Outlets 29

Implementing The Action Method...29

Connecting Action to Button 31

Chapter 4 - Using the SegmentedControl and WebView..........34

A Simple Photo Switcher App..34

Chapter 5 - Animating Images using Sliders..............................40

A Simple Animating Images App 40

Adding a Slider 46

Chapter 6 - Switching Between Views 50

Passing Values Between Views 54

What About Navigating Between Multiple Views? 62

Creating Segues 65

Chapter 7 - Using the TabBar Controller 71

Adding Another Tab 73

Chapter 8 - Creating TableViews 81

Designing The TableViewCell 87

UITableViewController Delegate Methods 90

Creating A Details View 92

Passing Values From The TableView to the Detailed View 98

Chapter 9 - Detecting Touches and Taps 101

Chapter 10 - Detecting Gestures 104

Chapter 11 - Building Location Based Apps 109

Displaying Annotations In Maps 117

Reverse Geo-Coding 119

Chapter 12 - Taking Photos and Accessing Photo Library 122

Chapter 13 - Accessing the Address Book 127

Adding Delegates 129

Chapter 14 - Using the Accelerometer 131

Device Movement..**134**

Appendix A - Deploying your App to a Device........................136

Connecting Your iOS Device **136**

Setting Up a Developer Program Account with Xcode..................**137**

Deploying an App on to your Device **141**

Appendix B - Submitting to the App Store............................142

Author's Note 152

Introduction

Welcome! Congratulations to taking the first step to creating amazing iOS applications!

iOS is the largest platform available and this easy-to-follow book walks you through the development process step by step. This book explores everything from the simple basics to advanced aspects of iOS application development.

In it, we teach you how to download the tools, get Xcode up and running, code iOS applications, submit your app to the App Store and share your finished iOS apps with the world.

Who this book is written for

This book is written for the beginning iOS developer. It would be great if you have some basic background in programming. But if you don't, do not worry as I explain fundamental programming concepts from the ground up. If you still want a dedicated resource to the Swift programming language, drop me a mail at support@i-ducate.com for a beginner's guide to Swift.

How this book is structured

In this book, we break down iOS programming into smaller chunks which make individual chapters. Each chapter and its code examples are independent from those in earlier chapter so this gives you the flexibility to go directly to topics that you are interested in.

What tools do I need?

You will need a Mac capable of running Xcode. Additionally having a real iOS device would be useful.

Source Code

Just drop us an email at support@i-ducate.com and we will send all source code to you!

Contact

We look forward to hearing from you at support@i-ducate.com. Now wait no further and get started on your iOS development learning journey!

Chapter 1 - Getting Started

Downloading Xcode From The Apple Developer Website

Go to https://developer.apple.com/devcenter/ios/index.action

Register as an Apple developer if you do not have an account yet. As an Apple developer, you get access to many useful features, code, tutorials, forums in the Apple developer community.

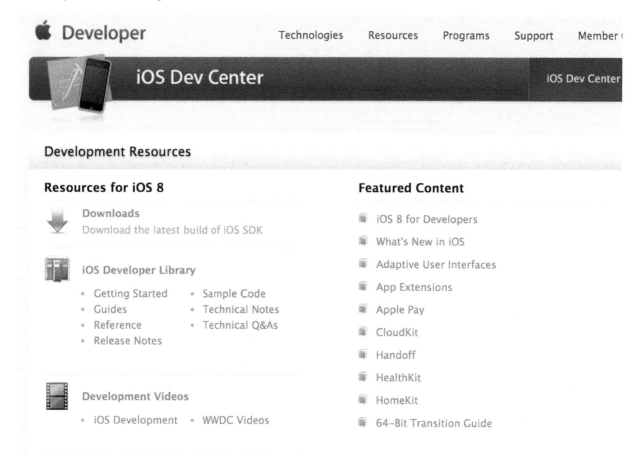

iOS Dev Center - Development Resources

Once you are logged in, Go to 'Downloads'

Downloads

Xcode 6.1

This is the complete Xcode developer toolset for Mac, iPhone, and iPad. It includes the Xcode IDE, iOS Simulator, and all required tools and frameworks for building OS X and iOS apps.

Download Xcode 6

Posted Date: Oct 20, 2014
Build: 6A1052d
Included iOS SDK: iOS 8.1
Included Mac SDK: OS X 10.10

iOS Dev Center - Download Xcode

You will see the latest version of Xcode. Download and install it. This will be the tool we will use to create our apps in the following sections.

Downloading Xcode From The Mac App Store

Alternatively, you can download Xcode from Apple Mac App Store -

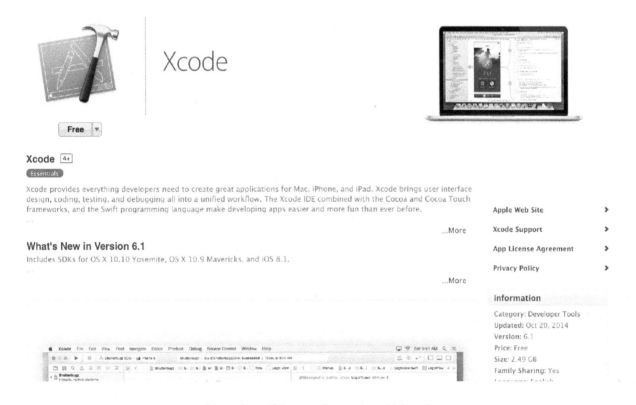

Mac App Store - Download Xcode

Overview of Xcode

In this section, we briefly introduce you to the Xcode interface. The below screenshot shows how a standard Xcode interface looks like with a newly created iOS project.

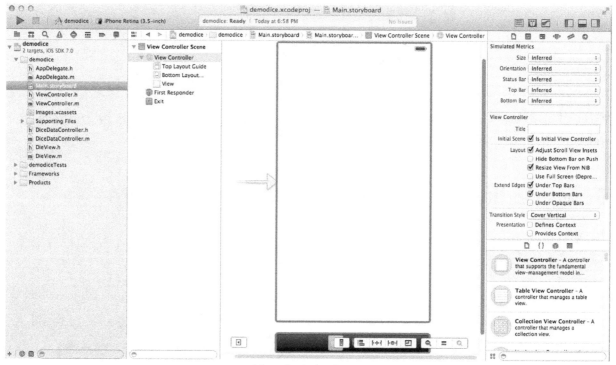

Xcode Interface

The project window has three main sections. The left section is the **Navigator pane** which shows a tree directory of all your project files.

The middle section is the **Editor pane** where you edit your project's source code or also build your user interfaces graphically.

The right section is the **Utilities pane** which contains inspectors that provide information about the current selection settings and lets you change them.

As you proceed through the following sections, you will learn how to create a project with Xcode and learn more about how to use Xcode better. Enjoy the journey!

Chapter 2 - Outlets and Actions (I)

A Simple Alert App

In this example, you will display a simple Alert message upon clicking a button. You will learn the basics of Actions here and will learn to connect a user interface element (like a button) to an Action.

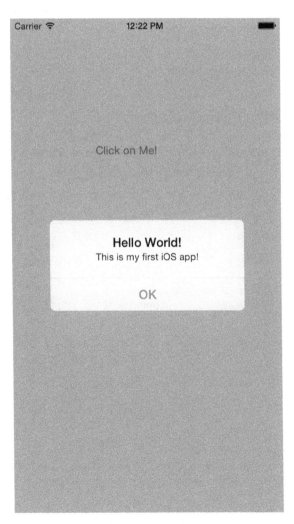

iPhone Simulator showing Simple Alert

First, open Xcode and you will see a welcome screen as follows -

Xcode Welcome Screen

From the Xcode welcome screen, select **Create a new Xcode project**. The next screen will prompt you to choose a template for your new project.

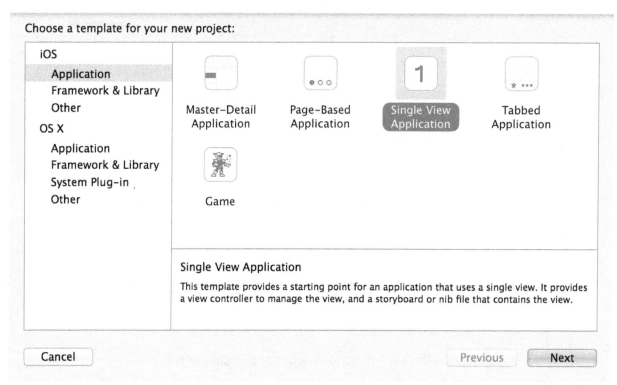

Choosing template for the new project

As you can see, there are a few different template types offered by Xcode. Based on your chosen template, Xcode will create a pre-configured project. This new project will include many source code files which are handy as a starting point.

Select **Single View Application** and press **Next**. This opens a new screen for you to enter options for your new app.

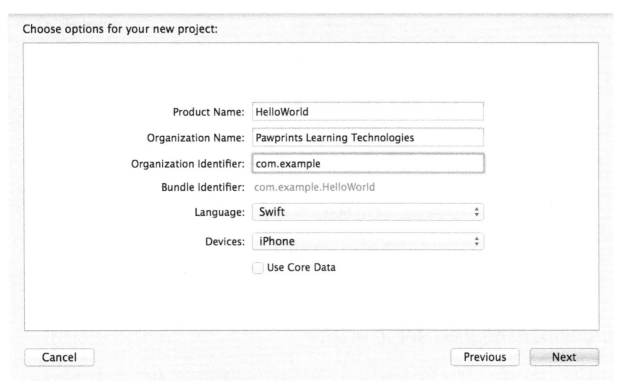

Choose options for your new project

Let me go through each of these options -

- **Product Name**: This is the name of your app. Enter '*HelloWorld*'.
- **Organization Name**: Enter your own name or name of your company.
- **Organization Identifier**: The Organization identifier is the domain name written in reverse order. If you own the domain *example.com*, you can use *com.example* as organization identifier. If you don't have a domain, you can pick something that seems unique to you or simply use your name. You can change this later.
- **Bundle Identifier**: This field is auto populated by combining the *Product Name* field and *Organisation Identifier* field.
- **Language**: Choose '*Swift*'
- **Devices**: Choose '*iPhone*'
- **Use Core Data**: Leave this *unchecked*

Press **Next**. Xcode will ask you where to save your project. Select any convenient location and press the **Create** button to finish the application creation process.

Xcode will automatically create a new folder for your project with the **Product Name** (*HelloWorld* in your case). The newly created project named *HelloWorld* will be opened in the Xcode project window.

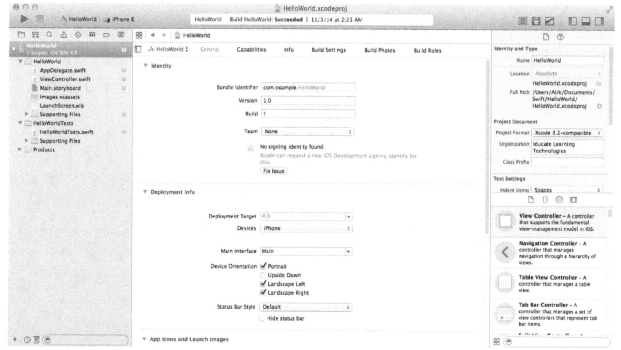

The Xcode window at the start of your project

Implementing the user interface

The left most pane of the Xcode window is named the **Navigator area**. You will see a row of icons at the top of the **Navigator area** that determines which navigator is visible. Currently, the first icon is selected, which is the **Project navigator**. This **Project navigator** shows a list of files that are part of your project.

From the **Project navigator**, find the file named *Main.storyboard* and click it once -

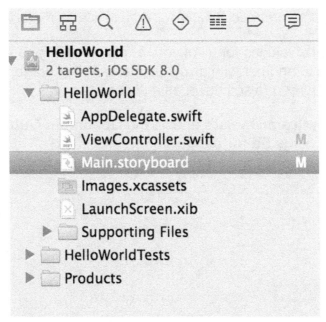

Select Main.storyboard from Project navigator

Once you select *Main.storyboard* from **Project navigator**, the **Editor pane** (middle pane) will show the **Interface Builder**. The **Interface Builder** tool lets you create components of your application visually, by drag-and-drop.

Your Xcode window should now look something like this -

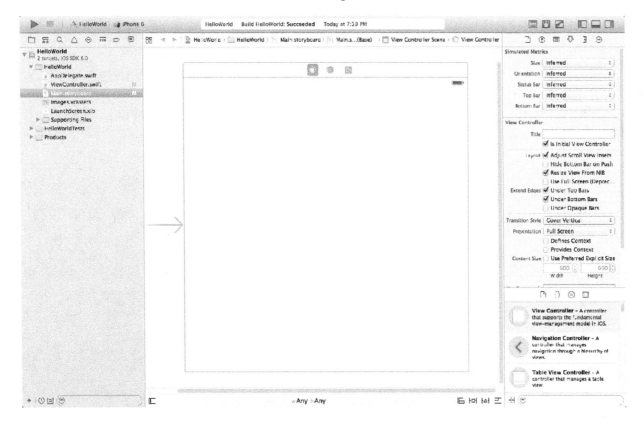

The storyboard contains designs for all of your app's screens and show how the app goes from one screen to another with arrow pointers. At this stage, the storyboard contains just a single screen (also known as a scene).

In order to see the view hierarchy, let's enable the **Document Outline** pane. Click the icon at the bottom-left of the **Editor pane**.

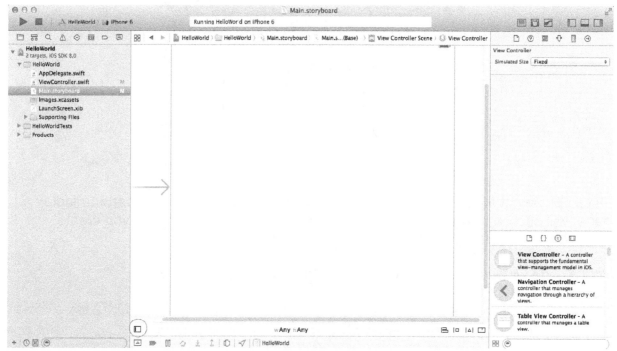

Click on show Document Outline icon (circled red)

Clicking on that icon will reveal the **Document Outline** pane at the right side of the **Navigator pane**.

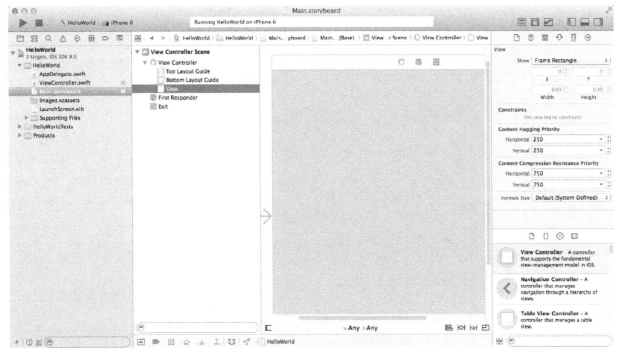

View Controller Scene hierarchy

From the view controller scene hierarchy, you can see that there is only a single screen. This screen is created as part of the new project creation process and is currently empty.

At this point, click the **Run** button located at the top-left corner -

Click the run button to launch app in iOS simulator

If this is the first time you are using Xcode, you will be prompted to enable 'developer mode'. Go ahead and click 'Enable' and then enter your password to allow Xcode to make these changes.

Xcode will build your application and launch in the iOS simulator -

iPhone Simulator running app with empty screen

The app doesn't look impressive at this stage because you haven't done anything yet except creating an empty project based on a template. But this is obviously an important step for you, because you just ran your very first iOS app! Congratulations!

You will be running most of your applications in the Simulator. But certain features like the GPS and Accelerometer features cannot be tested in the Simulator (you can't tilt your Mac right?!).

Before you move to the next section, press the **Stop** button (next to **Run** button) to stop the running app -

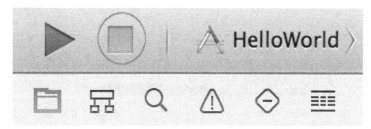

Stop running app

Building our View

Let's work on our currently empty view now. You might have noticed that the current empty view doesn't look like an iPhone screen. Rather it's more like a rectangle screen.

To fix that, select *Main.storyboard* from **Project navigator** pane and then select the **File Inspector** (the first icon) from **Utilities pane**. Scroll through the items and find the section **Interface Builder Document**. Then uncheck the option "Use Size Classes".

Disable Size Classes

Let's now concentrate on building our view. At the bottom of the **Utilities pane**, you will find the **Object Library** (make sure the third icon is selected, the one that looks like a circle).

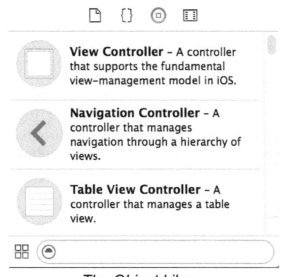

The Object Library

Scroll through the items in the **Object Library** until you see **Button**. Click on **Button** and drag it into the view.

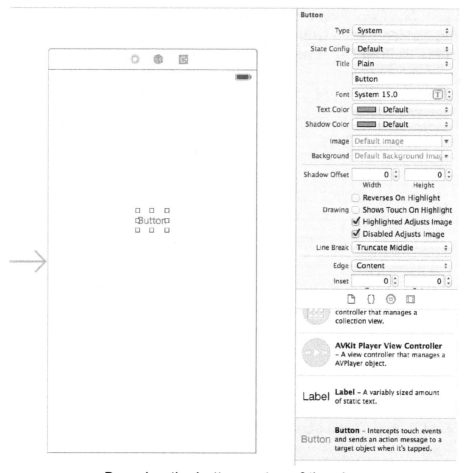

Dragging the button on top of the view

If you select the **Button** from the view, the **Attributes Inspector** (fourth icon from left) of **Utilities pane** will allow you to change different properties of the button, like title, font, text color and even image.

You can play with different properties and see how it looks. But for now, we are just going to change the button text. You can use **Attributes Inspector** to change the **Title** property of the button, Alternatively, double click on the button in the view and input the text 'Click on Me!'.

At this point, if you click the **Run** button in the Xcode's toolbar, the simulator will launch your app, which will look something like this -

Carrier 🖧   10:15 AM   ▬

Click on Me!

App running on iPhone 6 simulator

You can see that the 'Click on Me!' button appears on the screen. However, when you tap the button, it doesn't do anything yet. For that, you will need to write some Swift code!

Adding some Swift code

In the previous section, we added a button to our view. We want to show an alert message when a user taps the button. Let's add some Swift code to accomplish this. From **Project navigator**, find the *ViewController.swift* file and click once. The editor area will show the content of *ViewController.swift* file (this file is also automatically created as part of 'Single View Application' project creation).

In the *ViewController.swift* file, find the following code line -

class ViewController: UIViewController {

You will insert some Swift code immediately after the above line. Following are the lines of code you will need to add -

@IBAction func **showAlert() {**

```
    let alertController = UIAlertController(title: "Hello World!", message: "This is my first
iOS app!", preferredStyle: UIAlertControllerStyle.Alert)
    alertController.addAction(UIAlertAction(title: "OK", style: UIAlertActionStyle.Default,
handler: nil))
    presentViewController(alertController, animated: true, completion: nil)
  }
```

So, your *ViewController.swift* file should look like -

```
import UIKit

class ViewController: UIViewController {

  @IBAction func showAlert() {
    let alertController = UIAlertController(title: "Hello World!", message: "This is my first
iOS app!", preferredStyle: UIAlertControllerStyle.Alert)
    alertController.addAction(UIAlertAction(title: "OK", style: UIAlertActionStyle.Default,
handler: nil))
    presentViewController(alertController, animated: true, completion: nil)
  }

  override func viewDidLoad() {
    super.viewDidLoad()
    // Do any additional setup after loading the view, typically from a nib.
  }

  override func didReceiveMemoryWarning() {
    super.didReceiveMemoryWarning()
    // Dispose of any resources that can be recreated.
  }

}
```

Explanation

We added a new method named "showAlert" (this is also known as an 'Action'). The code in showAlert() method creates an alert with the title "Hello World", a message "This is my first iOS app!" and a single button labeled "OK". We do this in two steps, first we create an *UIAlertController* instance with title and message, which is assigned to a constant named *alertController* -

let alertController = UIAlertController(title: "Hello World!", message: "This is my first iOS app!", preferredStyle: UIAlertControllerStyle.Alert)

In the second step, we add a button titled "OK" by calling the *addAction()* method -

alertController.addAction(UIAlertAction(title: "OK", style: UIAlertActionStyle.Default, handler: nil))

Then we call *presentViewController()* method to make the alert message visible to screen -

presentViewController(alertController, animated: true, completion: nil)

Now, we want this showAlert() method to be executed automatically when user taps the button. We are just one step away from that. We just need to connect our button with our code!

Connecting our Button to Code

We need to establish a connection between our "Click on Me!" button and the showAlert() action. When someone taps the button, the app will respond by executing showAlert() method and show an alert message.

Select the *Main.storyboard* and click once. It will load the interface builder on to the editor pane. While pressing and holding the control key on your keyboard, click the "Click on Me!" button and drag it to the View Controller icon.

Release the mouse button first and then release the control button. You will see a pop-up with a few options. Select "showAlert" option under **Sent Events**. This will make a connection between the button and showAlert() action.

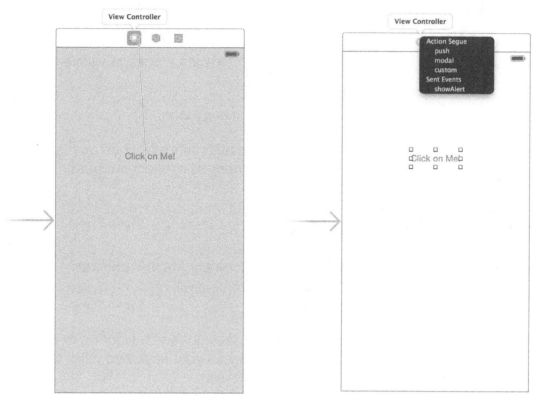

Drag to the View Controller icon (left) and a pop-over menu appears when releasing the button (right)

Explanation

We have connected our button to the showAlert() action. Whenever a user touches the button, an alert will now be shown.

Running the app

Click the **Run** button from Xcode's toolbar and the simulator will launch your app. If you click on the button, an alert box will be displayed -

Running HelloWorld app

As you can see, the alert has the title "Hello World!" and the text "This is my first iOS app!". If you click the 'OK' button, the alert disappear.

Learning Points

Congratulations! You have learned how to implement an 'Action' that shows an alert and connected that action to a button. Actions are used to trigger code when a specific user interaction occurs (i.e. pressing of a button). Go on to the next chapter to further your understanding in 'Actions' and also learn about 'Outlets'.

Chapter 3 - Outlets and Actions (II)

A Simple Calculator App

In this section, you will create a simple Calculator app that calculates the area of a circle.

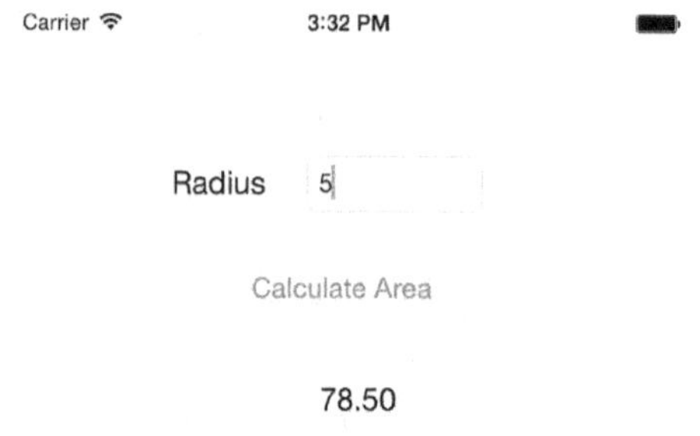

Carrier 🔋   3:32 PM

Radius   5

Calculate Area

78.50

A simple app for calculating area

Create a new Single View application and name it *SimpleCalculator*

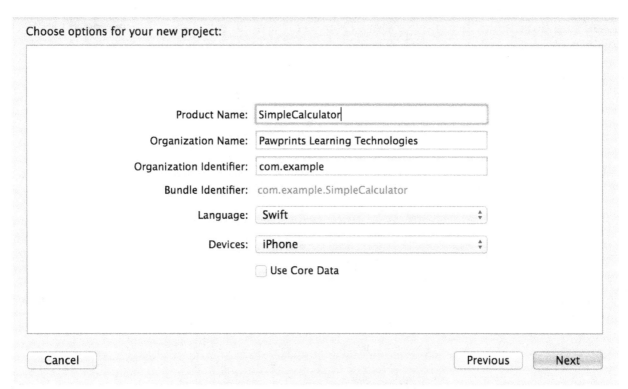

Choose options for your new project:

Product Name:	SimpleCalculator
Organization Name:	Pawprints Learning Technologies
Organization Identifier:	com.example
Bundle Identifier:	com.example.SimpleCalculator
Language:	Swift
Devices:	iPhone
	☐ Use Core Data

Cancel   Previous   Next

Options for creating new application

We will start by putting the necessary UI controls into the View. From the **Project navigator**, select *Main.storyboard* file and click it once. Now, from the Object Library, drag and drop a **Label** and change the text to 'Radius'.

Next, drag and drop in a **Text Field**.

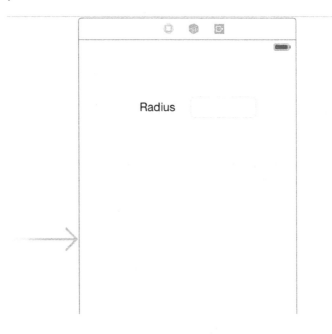

Radius

User interface with a Label and Text Field

Drag and drop a **Button** into the view. Double click on it to rename the text as 'Calculate Area'.

Add 'Calculate Area' button to user interface

We need one more UI control - a label for showing the calculated area. Place a **Label** into the view under the button. Double click on it and remove the text of the label.

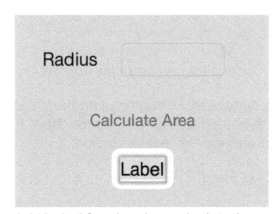

Add Label for showing calculated area

Now we should have all the necessary UI controls placed into our View.

Adding Outlets

In our app, a user will enter the value of radius into the Text Field and touch the 'Calculate Area' button. The user will expect to see the calculated area outputted on the Label.

So far, we only added necessary UI controls (or views) in Interface Builder. Now we need to be able to programmatically reference these views in code and also need to handle the touch event of the button. As you learned in the previous chapter, we handle events by using actions. Actions are very much like methods, which are annotated with the *IBAction* keyword.

To reference different views from our code, we use *Outlets*. An outlet is like a regular object property, which is annotated with the *IBOutlet* keyword.

28

In this application, we need to access two views programmatically - the **Text Field** for accessing the value of radius and the **Label** for displaying calculated area. So, we need to define the following two outlets in our *ViewController.swift* file -

@IBOutlet weak var **radiusTextField**: UITextField!
@IBOutlet weak var **areaLabel**: UILabel!

Add the above two lines of code immediately after the following line -

class ViewController: UIViewController {

Connecting the Outlets

Outlets represent pointers to the UI Controls. We now need to link the Outlets to the UI Controls that we have dragged on to the view.

Let's first connect the *radiusTextField* Outlet to the **Text Field**. Holding the Control key, mouse click and drag from the View Controller to the **Text Field** and select 'radiusTextField'. Note that, the direction of the drag is opposite to the connecting of button to an action.

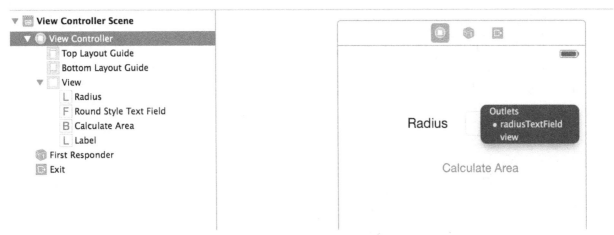

Connecting Text Field with outlets

Do the same for the *areaLabel* Outlet. Holding on the Control key, mouse click and drag from the View Controller to the Invisible label (we deleted the name just now) and select on 'areaLabel'.

Implementing The Action Method

At this point, both the Outlets are connected to corresponding UI Controls and we can now reference them from code. Next, we need to implement an action which will be triggered when a user touches the 'Calculate Area' button.

In your *ViewController.swift* file, add the following code immediately after the lines where you added Outlets -

```
@IBAction func calculateArea(sender: AnyObject) {
    var radiusStr : NSString = radiusTextField.text
    let pi : Double  = 3.14
    let radius = radiusStr.doubleValue
    let area = pi * radius * radius
    areaLabel.text = String(format: "%.2f", area)
}
```

The above code defines an action named 'calculateArea'. The *ViewController.swift* file should have the following code -

```
import UIKit

class ViewController: UIViewController {

  @IBOutlet weak var radiusTextField: UITextField!
  @IBOutlet weak var areaLabel: UILabel!

  @IBAction func calculateArea(sender: AnyObject) {
    var radiusStr : NSString = radiusTextField.text
    let pi : Double  = 3.14
    let radius : Double = radiusStr.doubleValue
    let area : Double = pi * radius * radius
    areaLabel.text = String(format: "%.2f", area)
  }

  override func viewDidLoad() {
    super.viewDidLoad()
    // Do any additional setup after loading the view, typically from a nib.
  }

  override func didReceiveMemoryWarning() {
    super.didReceiveMemoryWarning()
    // Dispose of any resources that can be recreated.
  }

}
```

Explanation

```
var radiusStr : NSString = radiusTextField.text
```

Declare a variable named *radiusStr* of type *NSString*. In Swift, we use the *var* keyword to declare a variable, which is followed by a variable name. After the variable name, we use colon (:) , followed by *type* of the variable to specify the data type. We want to get the value of radius entered into the Text Field which is done by using the *text* property of *radiusTextField*. This value is assigned to the variable *radiusStr* as a *NSString* type (which is just a string of characters). We will later get the numerical value of radius from this string representation.

```
let pi : Double  = 3.14
```

This line declares a constant named *pi* of type *Double* and assigns the value 3.14. Declaring constant in Swift is similar to declaring variable, you use the keyword *let* instead of using *var*.

```
let radius : Double = radiusStr.doubleValue
```

The above line gets the numeric value of radius from the variable *radiusStr* and assigns that to the constant named *radius*. Since user can enter radius with decimal point, we store the radius value as *Double* type.

```
let area : Double = pi * radius * radius
```

Next, we calculate the area using the formula *pi * radius * radius* and assign that to the constant named *area*.

```
areaLabel.text = String(format: "%.2f", area)
```

Finally, we output the calculated area by setting the *text* property of label *areaLabel*. While outputting the area, we format the value into a String with a format of two decimal places.

Instead of declaring constants for holding value of radius, area etc., we could have declared them as variables. But in Swift, we usually use constants for storing values that doesn't change.

Connecting Action to Button

We have defined the 'calculateArea' action, now we need to connect that with the button control. Select the *Main.storyboard* file from navigator area and single click to open it in editor pane. Next, holding on to Control key, click on the 'Calculate Area' button from interface builder and drag from the button to the View Controller (be careful to get the direction right!).

Select 'calculateArea' in the pop up menu -

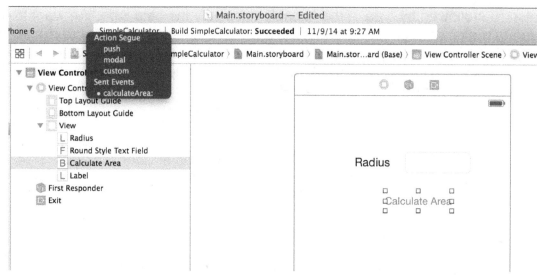

Connecting action with button

Running Application

Now we are ready to run the application. Click the **Run** button from the top menu of Xcode and the app should run in the Simulator.

Enter radius into the text field and click 'Calculate Area' button. The calculated area should appear onto the label -

Carrier 🗢   3:32 PM   ▬

Radius   5|

Calculate Area

78.50

Congratulations! You have developed your own SimpleCalculator app.

What you have learned

You have learned the basics of declaring Outlets to refer to UI controls. You have learned how to define and implement Action method to connect to a button. You have learned how to take user input and output calculated results to a label. This is a powerful concept and you can go on to add more text boxes and labels for more comprehensive views (eg. name, address, phone) to take in more user input.

Chapter 4 - Using the SegmentedControl and WebView

A Simple Photo Switcher App

In this section, you will learn how to create an app that switches photos with a Segmented control. Further, the photo will be retrieved from a remote website.

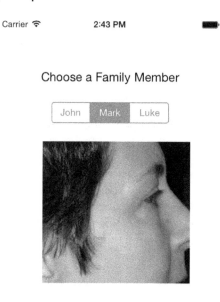

Figure: Running PhotoSwitcher app

Create a new Single View iPhone application and name it as *PhotoSwitcher*. Next, add a label and a Segmented Control to your view. Double click on the label and change the text to "Choose a Family Member".

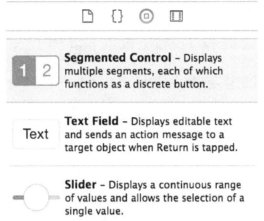

Figure: Select Segmented Control from Object Library

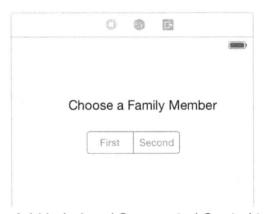

Figure: Add Label and Segmented Control to View

Select the Segmented Control. Under the 'Attribute Inspector' of the Segmented Control, change the value under Segments to 3. Under the *Title*, enter the title of each of the segment. Note that, the segments start from the index zero.

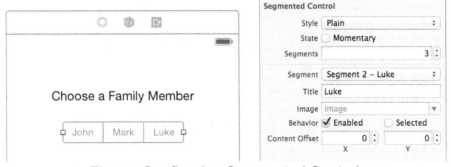

Figure: Configuring Segmented Control

Enter John for segment 0, Mark for segment 1 and Luke for segment 2. Alternatively, you can enter your own family member names! Resize the control so that the text fits nicely.

Declare an Outlet for the SegmentedControl in *ViewController.swift* file by adding the following line immediately after the opening curly brace -

@IBOutlet weak var memberChoice: UISegmentedControl!

Connect the Outlet to the SegmentedControl in Interface Builder by holding on Ctrl and drag click from *View Controller* to Segmented Control and select *memberChoice* -

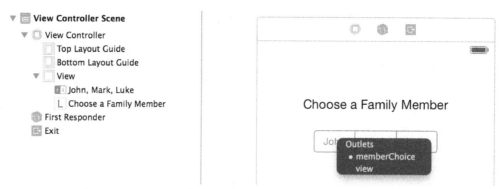

Figure: Connecting Outlet to the SegmentedControl

Now, add a WebView under the Segmented Control to display the various photos.

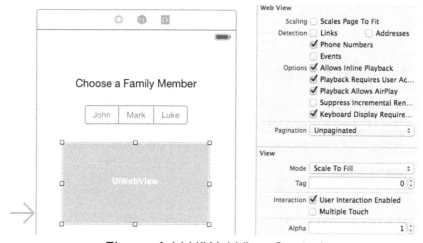

Figure: Add UIWebView Control

Next, you need to declare an Outlet for the WebView. Add the following line to your *ViewController.swift* file -

@IBOutlet weak var webView: UIWebView!

Then, connect the Outlet to the WebView by holding on Ctrl and drag click from *View Controller* to WebView and select *webView* -

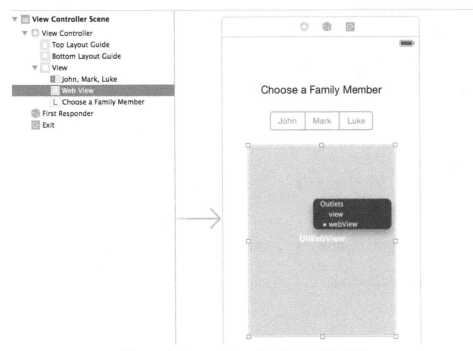

Figure: Connecting Outlet to WebView

Next, you need to add the following *getMember* action method in your *ViewController.swift* file -

```
@IBAction func getMember(sender: AnyObject) {
    var member: String =
memberChoice.titleForSegmentAtIndex(memberChoice.selectedSegmentIndex)!
    var imageURLString: String!

    if member == "John" {
        imageURLString = "http://s27.postimg.org/ik6bvknwj/001.jpg"
    }
    else if member == "Mark" {
        imageURLString = "http://s4.postimg.org/3mqub6rnh/002.jpg"
    }
    else if member == "Luke" {
        imageURLString = "http://s23.postimg.org/63spg2zo7/003.jpg"
    }

    var imageURL: NSURL = NSURL(string: imageURLString)
    webView.loadRequest(NSURLRequest(URL: imageURL))
}
```

Finally, connect the SegmentedControl to the action by holding on Ctrl and drag click to the *View Controller*. Select *getMember*.

Figure: Connecting action to Segmented Control

Click on Run and your app should run on simulator -

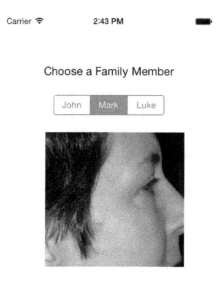

Figure: Running App on Simulator

When you click on a segment, the photo of that segment fetches an image of that family member into the *WebView*. Remeber to resize the *WebView* so that your photo can fit nicely into the *WebView*.

Explanation of getMember Action Method

var member: String =
memberChoice.titleForSegmentAtIndex(memberChoice.selectedSegmentIndex)!

In the above code, we declare a variable member to store the value of the selected segment's title.

```
var imageURLString: String!

    if member == "John" {
        imageURLString = "http://s27.postimg.org/ik6bvknwj/001.jpg"
    }
    else if member == "Mark" {
        imageURLString = "http://s4.postimg.org/3mqub6rnh/002.jpg"
    }
    else if member == "Luke" {
        imageURLString = "http://s23.postimg.org/63spg2zo7/003.jpg"
    }
```

Using an if-else-if statement, we check if the *member* variable has a value of either John, Mark or Luke. If its anyone of them, we go into the scope of that *if* condition and assign the image URL to the *imageURLString* variable.

var imageURL: NSURL = NSURL(string: imageURLString)
    webView.loadRequest(NSURLRequest(URL: imageURL))

Finally, we create an NSURL object with the imageURLString to load the image into our *WebView*. The NSURL object can be used to load any website as well.

Note that because we have linked the SegmentedControl to the Action getMember in Interface Builder, everytime a user clicks on the SegmentedControl, the getMember method is called.

What You have Learned

We have learned how to use the SegmentedControl and how to use the if-else-if selection statement to populate a remote image into a *WebView*.

Chapter 5 - Animating Images using Sliders

A Simple Animating Images App

In this section, you will learn how to animate multiple pictures in an *imageview* and having a button to start and stop the animation. In addition, you will learn how to use a slider control and edit the alpha (transparency) property of the animation.

Figure: Running completed app

Create a new Single View iPhone App and name it as *AnimatingImage*. Before we start adding UI controls, make sure you disable size classes (check previous chapter if you don't remember how to do that).

Now select *Main.storyboard* file from the project navigator and drag a button to the top. Change the button label to 'Animate'.

Next, add a *UIImageView* below the button element. Keep some space between the button and the *UIImageView*.

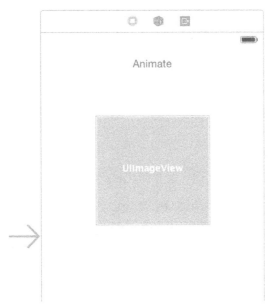

Figure: Add button and image view

Now declare two Outlets for *imageview* and button in *ViewController.swift* file -

```
import UIKit
class ViewController: UIViewController {
    @IBOutlet weak var imageView: UIImageView!
    @IBOutlet weak var runButton: UIButton!

    override func viewDidLoad() {
        super.viewDidLoad()
        // Do any additional setup after loading the view, typically from a nib.
    }
    override func didReceiveMemoryWarning() {
        super.didReceiveMemoryWarning()
        // Dispose of any resources that can be recreated.
    }

}
```

Connect the Outlets to the *imageView* and button

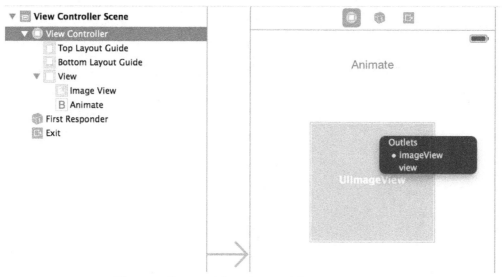

Figure: Connecting imageView with Outlet

Add three images into your project by right clicking on **Supporting Files > Add Files to … > browse select your files**. Make sure you keep the 'copy items if needed' checkbox checked. I have added pet_bird.png, pet_cat.png and pet_dog.png.

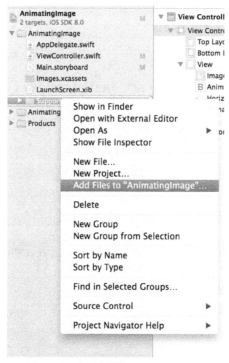

Figure: Add Files to project

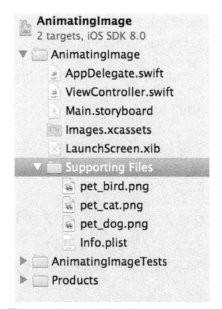

Figure: Importing image assets

Add in the below codes into the *viewDidLoad()* method of *ViewController.swift* file -

import UIKit

```
class ViewController: UIViewController {
    @IBOutlet weak var imageView: UIImageView!
    @IBOutlet weak var runButton: UIButton!

    override func viewDidLoad() {
        super.viewDidLoad()
        // Do any additional setup after loading the view, typically from a nib.

        var animationImages = [UIImage(named: "pet_bird.png"), UIImage(named:
"pet_cat.png"), UIImage(named: "pet_dog.png")]

        imageView.animationImages = animationImages
        imageView.animationDuration = 1
    }
    override func didReceiveMemoryWarning() {
        super.didReceiveMemoryWarning()
        // Dispose of any resources that can be recreated.
    }
}
```

Explanation

The *viewDidLoad()* method is called after the view has loaded while starting up. Within this method, we create an array that store the images that will animate -

var animationImages = [UIImage(named: "pet_bird.png"),
UIImage(named: "pet_cat.png"), UIImage(named: "pet_dog.png")]

Then we assign the array to the imageView's *animationImages* property -

imageView.animationImages = animationImages

Finally, we set the transition speed to be 1 sec between images -

imageView.animationDuration = 1

Implementing The Run Animation Method

Next, add the below codes to ViewController.swift file, immediately after Outlets declaration -

```
@IBAction func runAnimation(sender: UIButton) {
    if imageView.isAnimating() {
        imageView.stopAnimating()
        runButton.setTitle("Start!", forState: UIControlState.Normal)
    } else {
        imageView.startAnimating()
        runButton.setTitle("Stop!", forState: UIControlState.Normal)
    }
}
```

Explanation

The *runAnimation()* method is an action which will be linked to the button that starts and stops the animation. Within this method definition, we check whether the *imageView* is currently animating or not.

if imageView.isAnimating() {
    imageView.stopAnimating()
    runButton.setTitle("Start!", forState: UIControlState.Normal)
}

If the state of the *imageView* is animating, we stop the animation and set the title of the button to 'Start!', indicating that the next press of the button starts the animation again.

else {
    imageView.startAnimating()
    runButton.setTitle("Stop!", forState: UIControlState.Normal)
}

Else, the *imageView* is not animating. In that case, we start the animation and set the title of the button to 'Stop!', indicating the next press of the button stops the animation.

Connecting the Action to runAnimation

Link the button to the action and select the action '*runAnimation*'.

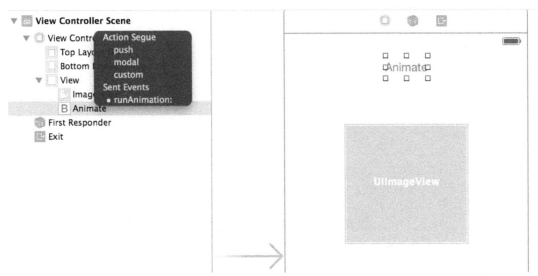

Figure: Connect Action to runAnimation

Run your project and you should see your images being animated when you press on 'Animate' and stop animating when you press the button again.

Figure: Animating images

Adding a Slider

We will be adding a slider bar to the animation app to change the alpha of the image view as the animation runs. The alpha is the transparency level of the image view.

Drag a slider from the object library and place it between the button and the image view.

Add two labels, one for displaying the text 'Alpha' and another one for displaying the current alpha value. Make sure the size of the label at the right of the slider can show decimal digits because we will show a decimal value there.

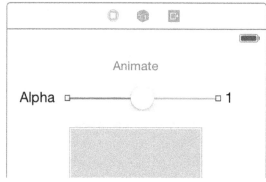

Figure: Adding slider and two labels

Add two more Outlets to *ViewController.swift* file - one for slider and another one for alpha value label -

@IBOutlet weak var alphaSlider: UISlider!
@IBOutlet weak var alphaLabel: UILabel!

Next, ensure that you connect the Outlets to them in the view. You should know how to do that by now! Else, please re-visit the earlier chapters.

Now, select the slider from the storyboard and go to attributes inspector. Set the minimum, maximum and current value of the slider as 0, 1 and 0.5 respectively.

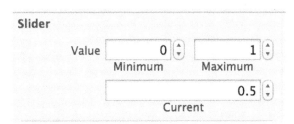

Figure: Setting attributes for slider

Now add the following action method to your *ViewController.swift* file -

@IBAction func setAlphaValue(sender: UISlider) {
    var alphaValue: String
    imageView.startAnimating()
    runButton.setTitle("Stop!", forState: UIControlState.Normal)
    imageView.alpha = CGFloat(alphaSlider.value)
    alphaValue = String(format: "%.2f", alphaSlider.value)
    alphaLabel.text = alphaValue
}

Link the slider to the action we have just created by holding control and click drag from the slider to the View Controller and select *setAlphaValue*.

Run the project and notice the alpha changes when you slide the slider.

Notice that your alpha label's value changes as well.

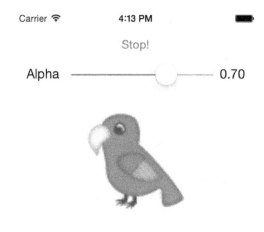

Figure: Running the application

Explanation

Since we have linked *setAlphaValue()* action method to the slider, when we slide, the *setAlphaValue()* method will be called.

   var alphaValue: String

The above statement declares a variable named *alphaValue* of type string.

imageView.startAnimating()

This line starts the animation.
runButton.setTitle("Stop!", forState: UIControlState.Normal)

When the animation starts, we want to change the button label to 'Stop!' so that a user can understand that clicking that button will stop the animation. The above code does exactly that.

imageView.alpha = CGFloat(alphaSlider.value)

The above statement sets the *alpha* property of *imageView* to the slider's value which is a decimal number between 0 and 1. We typecast that value to the *CGFloat* type.

alphaValue = String(format: "%.2f", alphaSlider.value)
alphaLabel.text = alphaValue

Display the alpha value in floating value up to 2 decimal places to the label and output this value in the alpha label.

What We have Learnt

We have learned how to animate images, change title of buttons depending on different states and learned how to use the slider.

Chapter 6 - Switching Between Views

In this section, you will learn how to switch between views. We will be utilizing the Storyboard function to design our views navigation.

Create a Single View Application and name it as *SwitchViewsApp*.

Figure: Create new project

So far, we have been using the Storyboard to design our application's views. But Storyboard offers more than that, it allows you to keep track of navigation links from one view to another.

From the project navigator, click the *Main.storyboard* file once. You should see one View Controller in the storyboard canvas. We will add additional View Controllers into the storyboard. Before that, make sure you disable size classes as usual.

Now drag a View Controller from the object library into the storyboard. It doesn't matter where you put your View Controllers within the storyboard. You might want to zoom out to facilitate positioning View Controllers. You can double click to zoom out.

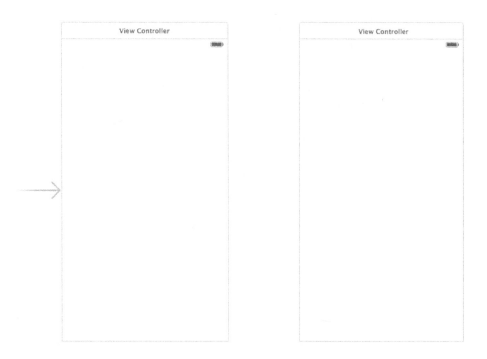

Figure: Add a new View Controller into storyboard

Now we will add UI controls into both views. You cannot drag UI controls into view when it is zoomed out, so zoom into the first view and drag a button into it. Rename the button to "Go To Next View". Similarly, add a button into the second view and rename it to "Go to Previous View". The buttons will be used to navigate between the two views.

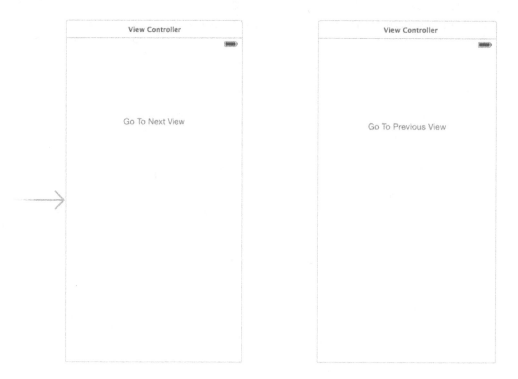

Figure: Add buttons to views

Next, control click from the button on the first view and drag it to the second view. The 'Action Segue' menu will pop up. Select 'modal' from the popup. A connecting line called a Segue between the two views will be generated.

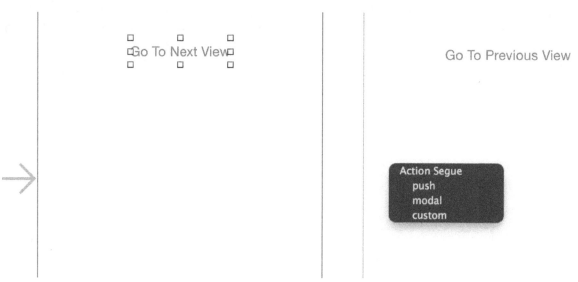

Figure: Selecting 'modal' action segue

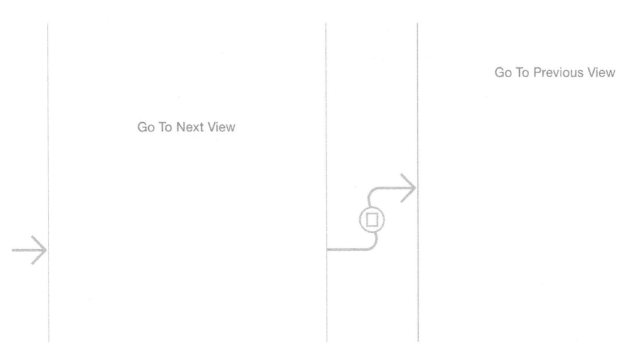

Figure: Segue from first view controller to second view controller

Note: There are other options like 'push' which is the kind of Segue you use when the two view controllers are inside a *UINavigationController*. But because our view controllers are not inside a *UINavigationController*, 'push' will do nothing. We will stick with 'modal' for now. We will introduce 'push' later.

Select the segue and go to the attribute inspector. From the '*Transition*' dropdown, select a transition animation. This will determine the animation transition between views.

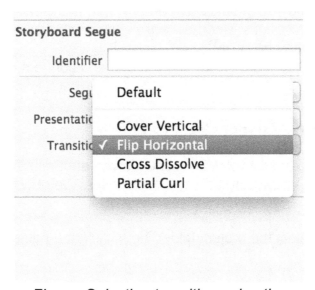

Figure: Selecting transition animation

Now, do the above steps for the second view. Start by control clicking from the button on the second view to the first view. Under the 'Action Segue', select 'modal'. Next, select the segue and from attribute inspector, choose a transition animation. At this stage, your storyboard should look something like this -

Go To Previous View

Go To Next View

Figure: Storyboard with two view controllers and segues between them

Depending upon the relative positions of the view controllers within your storyboard, the segues might look a bit different which is completely fine.

Now run your project and you should have an app with two views and you can navigate between them using the buttons. See how easy view navigation is within a storyboard? We have absolutely written no code!
Going further, you can add more views and buttons and connect them, linking them to one another!

Passing Values Between Views

Now, what if we need to pass values from one view to another? The original view already has the default ViewController.swift as its class. We now need to add class files for our Second View.

To add our class file, select the project folder, right click and select 'New File'.

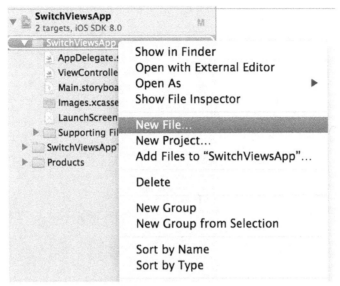

Figure: Add new file

The next screen will prompt you to choose a template for creating a new file. Select **iOS** → **Source** from the left panel and choose the **Cocoa Touch Class**.

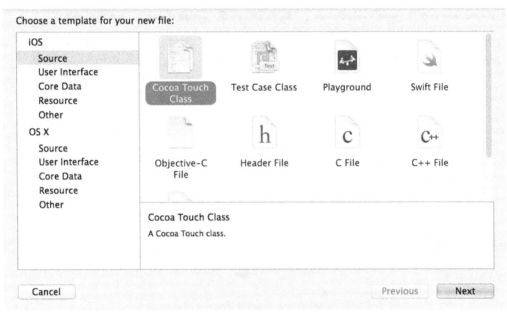

File: Selecting Cocoa Touch Class

Click the **Next** button and fill in the necessary fields as shown below -

Figure: Create SecondViewController class

Make sure you name the class as *SecondViewController*. Select *UIViewController* for subclass as field and select *Swift* as language. Click **Next**, the file named *SecondViewController.swift* will be generated in the project directory.

Figure: SecondViewController.swift file

To connect the *SecondViewController.swift* to the second view, go back to the storyboard and select the second view (make sure you click the first yellow icon at the top of the second view).

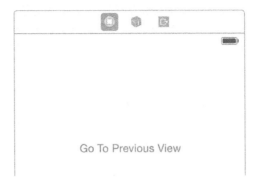

Figure: Selecting second view

Now go to the inspector pane and select Identity Inspector (third icon from left). In class field, select *SecondViewController.* Once you have done that, the *SecondViewController.swif* file acts as the class for the second view.

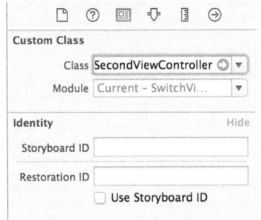

Figure: Select class for second view

Now go back to storyboard and add a new text field in the first view. We will allow the user to enter a message in the text field and pass the message over to the second view controller.

Figure: Add text field to first view

In the second view, add a label. This label will output the message passed from the first view.

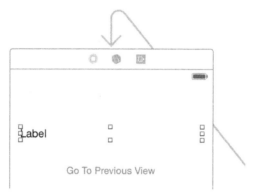

Figure: Add label to second view

In *ViewController.swift*, add the codes in bold below, which declares an Outlet for text field and add a method to pass data to the second view. Remember to connect the Outlet to the text field in your storyboard.

```
import UIKit

class ViewController: UIViewController {

    @IBOutlet weak var textField: UITextField!

    override func viewDidLoad() {
    super.viewDidLoad()
    // Do any additional setup after loading the view, typically from a nib.
    }

    override func didReceiveMemoryWarning() {
```

```
    super.didReceiveMemoryWarning()
    // Dispose of any resources that can be recreated.
}

override func prepareForSegue(segue: UIStoryboardSegue, sender: AnyObject?) {
var secondViewController = segue.destinationViewController as SecondViewController
secondViewController.message = textField.text
}

}
```

Explanation

@IBOutlet weak var textField: UITextField!

The above line declares an Outlet for the text field.

override func prepareForSegue(segue: UIStoryboardSegue, sender: AnyObject?) {

The *prepareForSegue* method is called when the Segue is performed. That is to say, when the transition from the first view to the second view happens. It is thus useful for us to transfer values between views.

var secondViewController = segue.destinationViewController as SecondViewController

Within the *prepareForSegue* method, we retrieve the reference of the second view controller with the above code. The *destinationViewController* of *segue* object returns an instance of *UIViewController*, which we typecast to *SecondViewController* using the '*as*' keyword.

secondViewController.message = textField.text

Finally, we assign the text in the *textField* to the *message* variable in the *secondViewController*. We have not declared the message variable yet so Xcode will give you an error. But that's fine, we will fix that soon.

SecondViewController

In *SecondViewController.swift*, add the codes below. We declared the Outlet for the label in the second view. Remember to connect the Outlet to the label in the second view.

We also declare a String property *message* which will store the string value passed from the first view to the second view.

import UIKit

```
class SecondViewController: UIViewController {

    @IBOutlet weak var messageLabel: UILabel!
    var message: String!

    override func viewDidLoad() {
    super.viewDidLoad()

    messageLabel.text = message
    }

    override func didReceiveMemoryWarning() {
    super.didReceiveMemoryWarning()
    // Dispose of any resources that can be recreated.
    }

}
```

Explanation

@IBOutlet weak var messageLabel: UILabel!

This line declares an Outlet for the label.

var message: String!

We declare a variable named *message* which is of type String. This variable will hold the value of the string passed from the first view.

messageLabel.text = message

This line is called within the *viewDidLoad()* method and set the text property of *messageLabel* to the value stored in the variable *message*. The value of the variable *message* is set from *prepareForSegue()* method of *ViewController.swift* class.

Running The App

Run the app now. You should be able to enter a message in the first view and see the message in the label in second view by clicking the button.

Congratulations! You have learned how to transfer values between views!

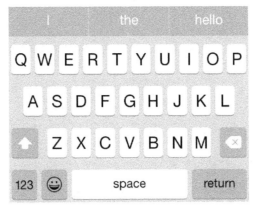

Figure: Running app – entering text in first view's text field

I love iOS Programming!

Go To Previous View

Figure: Running the app – text entered in first view appears to second view

What About Navigating Between Multiple Views?

So far, we have illustrated navigation between two views and using the segue to pass values from one view to another. But what about when we have to navigate between multiple views and passing values to the correct view?

To illustrate this, we will be adding one more button to our first view which will navigate to a third view. We will also be passing the string in the text field to the third view as what we have done in the second view.

Getting Started

First, add another button in the first view and rename it as "Go To Third View".

View Controller

Go To Next View

Go To Third View

Figure: Add new button to first view

Next, in the storyboard, add a new View Controller, which will be our third view.

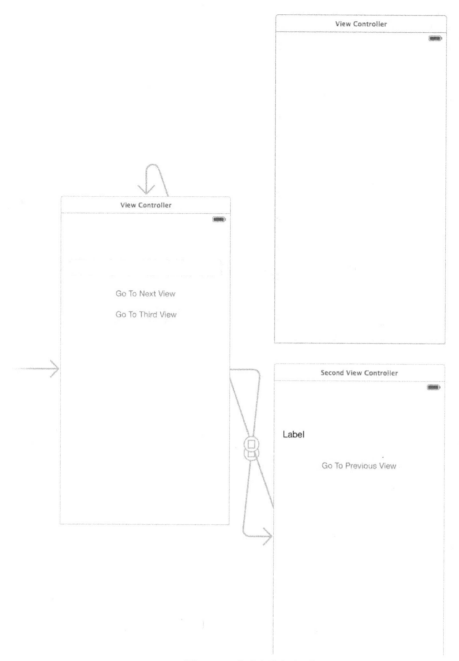

Figure: Add third view controller

Next, to distinguish the third view from the second view, change the background color of the view to yellow (or any favorite color!). To change the background color of the view, you need the select the third view controller and go to attribute inspector. Then find the background color property and change that to your desired color.

Once you change the background color of third view, add a label and a button to it the same way you did for the second view. Change the button label to "Return To Previous View".

Creating Segues

Now, create a segue by control-clicking from the 'Go To Third View' button in the first view to the third view. Select 'modal' from *Action Segue* popup. Next, create a segue by control clicking from the 'Return To Previous View' button in third view to the first view.

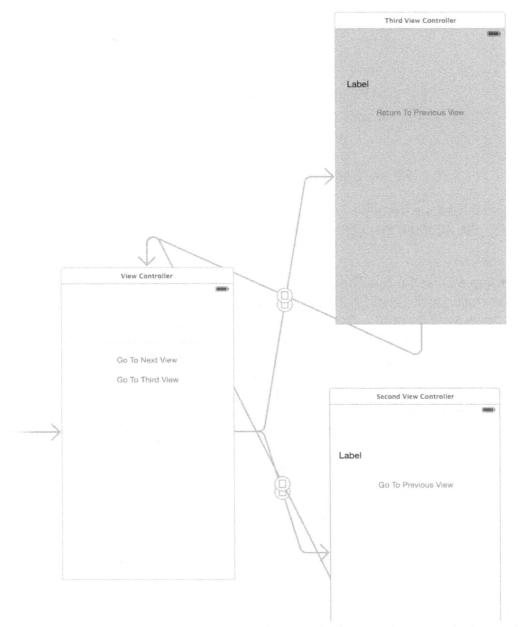

Figure: Storyboard with three view controllers and segues between them

Giving the Segue Identifiers

Now, select the Segue from the first view's "Go To Third View" button at the third view and go to the attribute inspector. Here you will set an identifier for the segue. Enter

'ThirdViewSegue' as the value of *Identifier* field. In our code, we can now identify this segue as 'ThirdViewSegue'. So you see, we can identify each segue by its identifier and thus control specific actions to perform for each segue.

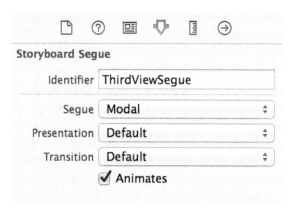

Figure: Setting identifier for segue

We will next give the segue from the first view button to the second view. Click on that segue and under the attribute inspector, enter the value 'SecondViewSegue' for the *Identifier* field.

We will next create a class for the Third view. This is similar to creating the *SecondViewController.swift* class for the second view. Create the class *ThirdViewController.swift* by right clicking project directory and selecting **New File →
iOS → Source → Cocoa Touch Class**. Make sure you name the **class** as *ThirdViewController.* Select *UIViewController* for **subclass as** field and select *Swift* as **language**.

Then connect the class to the third view. Start by selecting the third view controller from the storyboard and then go to the identity inspector. Then select the *ThirdViewController* as the value of **Class** field.

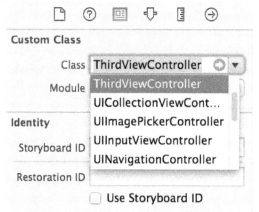

Figure: Setting class for third view

ThirdViewController

Update the *ThirdViewController.swift* file with the following code which creates the Outlet for the label and a variable named *message* of type string to store the message just as what we have done for *SecondViewController.swift.* Also remember to connect the Outlet to the label in the storyboard.

import UIKit

class ThirdViewController: UIViewController {

   @IBOutlet weak var messageLabel: UILabel!
   var message: String!

   override func viewDidLoad() {
     super.viewDidLoad()

     messageLabel.text = message
  }

   override func didReceiveMemoryWarning() {
     super.didReceiveMemoryWarning()
     // Dispose of any resources that can be recreated.
  }

}

Explanation

@IBOutlet weak var messageLabel: UILabel!

This line declares an Outlet for the label.

var message: String!

We declare a variable named *message* which is of type String. This variable will hold the value of the string passed from the first view.

messageLabel.text = message

This line is called within the *viewDidLoad()* method and set the text property of *messageLabel* to the value stored in the variable *message*. The value of the variable *message* is set from *prepareForSegue()* method of *ViewController.swift* class.

ViewController

Update your ViewController.swift file's prepareForSegue method with the following code -

```
override func prepareForSegue(segue: UIStoryboardSegue, sender: AnyObject?) {
    if segue.identifier == "SecondViewSegue" {
        var secondViewController = segue.destinationViewController as
SecondViewController
        secondViewController.message = textField.text
    }
    else if segue.identifier == "ThirdViewSegue" {
        var thirdViewController = segue.destinationViewController as
ThirdViewController
        thirdViewController.message = textField.text
    }
}
```

Explanation

Remember that we gave identifiers to our segues previously? We now use these segue identifiers in a if-else statement to determine what actions to perform when a particular segue is triggered.

```
if segue.identifier == "SecondViewSegue" {
    var secondViewController = segue.destinationViewController as
SecondViewController
    secondViewController.message = textField.text
}
```

The above code checks if the segue identifier is 'SecondViewSegue' and if so, we retrieve an instance of *SecondViewController* from the segue object. We then assign the text from the text field to the message property of the *secondViewController* instance.

```
else if segue.identifier == "ThirdViewSegue" {
    var thirdViewController = segue.destinationViewController as  ThirdViewController
    thirdViewController.message = textField.text
}
```

In this case, we check if the segue's identifier is 'ThirdViewSegue'. If that's the case, we do the same thing but for *ThirdViewController*.

Running The App

Run the app and upon typing a message, click on the 'Go To Third View' button and notice that, your message is displayed in the third view. If you press on the 'Go To Next View' button instead, you will be directed to the second view.

Hello Third View!

Go To Next View

Go To Third View

Figure: Running app

Figure: Navigate to third view

What You Have Learnt

Congratulations! You now have the necessary skills to implement more complex view navigation and pass values between them.

Chapter 7 - Using the TabBar Controller

In this section, you will learn how to use the *TabBar* controller. We will be utilizing the Storyboard function to design our TabBar views.

Create a 'Tabbed Application' iPhone app and name it as *TabBarApp*.

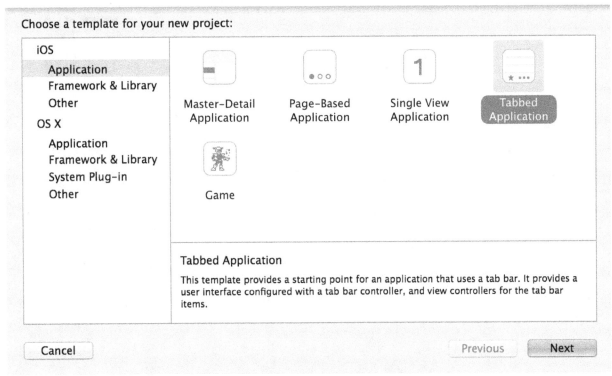

Figure: Creating Tabbed Application

Note that with the creation of Tabbed Application, you have two view controller classes – *FirstViewController.swift* and *SecondViewController.swift*. Click on *Main.storyboard* file and disable size classes. Your storyboard should look something like this -

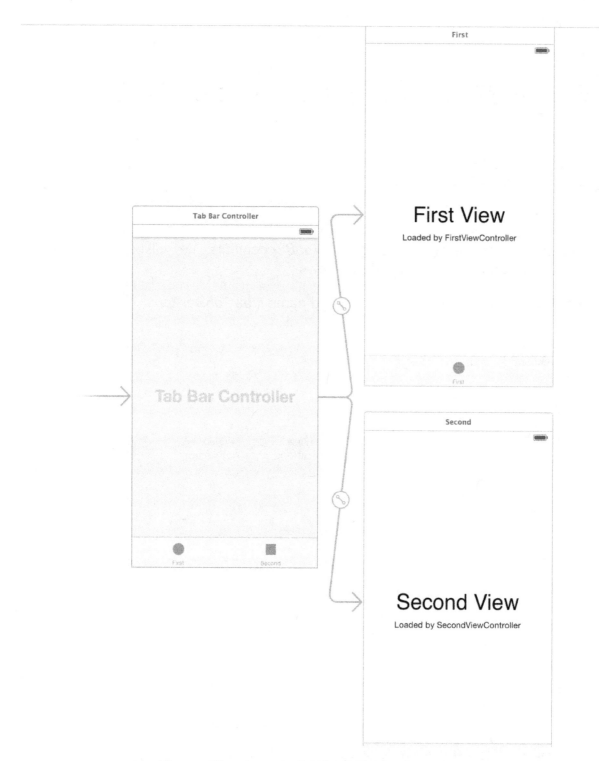

Figure: Storyboard of default Tabbed application

As you can guess from the name, the *Tabbed Application* consist of multiple '*tabs*' (or views). By default, the *Tabbed Application* template has two views. The *FirstViewController.swift* is linked to the first view and the *SecondViewController.swift* is linked to the second view. These two views are managed by a *UITabBarController* class. If you take a look at the above storyboard image, you will see a Tab Bar

Controller which is followed by an arrow. That arrow indicates that the first view which will be loaded when you run your application.

The Tab Bar Controller acts as a container for other views. As soon as a Tab Bar Controller loads, it will immediately load the first view. The Tab Bar Controller provides a tab bar at the bottom of all of the views that it manages. You can navigate to those views by clicking the corresponding tab bar items. The two views created with the default tab bar application are automatically connected to the Tab Bar Controller. That is why you can see the connecting segues in the storyboard.

At this stage, you can run the application and can navigate to the first and second views by clicking the tab bar items.

You can add any UI Control items (like buttons, text fields, labels etc) to either of these two views.

In the next section, you will see how we can add a third view and connect that to tab bar controller, so that we have three tabs.

Adding Another Tab

We currently have only two tabs in the TabBarApp. Let's add one more tab connecting to a third view. Once you have mastered this, you can do the same to add on multiple views.

In the zoomed out storyboard, drag a 'View Controller' into the canvas.

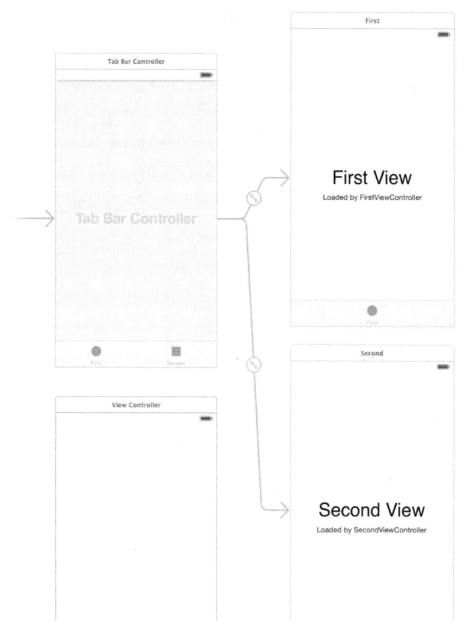

Figure: Add new view controller

Next, control click and drag from the Tab Bar Controller to the new View Controller you just added.

A popup will appear. Select 'view controllers' under the *Relationship Segue*.

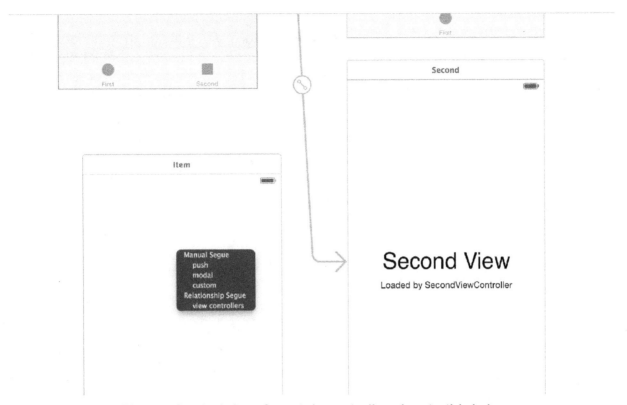

Figure: Control drag from tab controller view to third view

Once you have done that, a line connecting a third tab (auto-generated) from the Tab Bar Controller view to the third view will be generated.

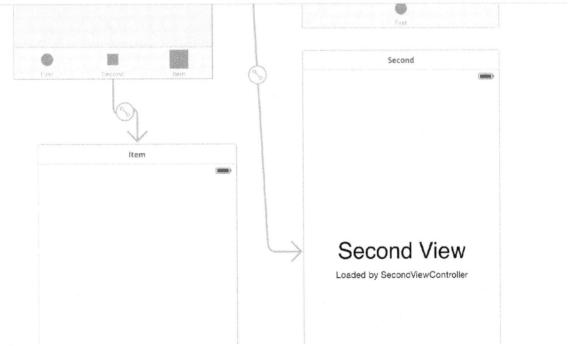

Figure: Create relationship segue

Yes, its that easy! If you take a look at the above picture, you will see that the label of third tab is 'Item'. We want to change that to 'Third'. In order to change that label, you need to select the Third View's tab bar item and go to the attributes inspector. Under the Bar Item, change the title field to *Third*.

Figure: Change bar item title

As soon as you change that, the label of third tab bar item will be changed to 'Third'.

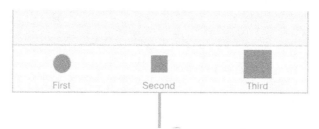

Figure: Label of third tab bar item changed

You can even set a custom image for the tab bar item from the same attribute inspector area. The image attribute is immediately below the title attribute -

Figure: Set image for tab bar item

Next we have to create a ViewController class for the code of the third View Controller. Right click the TabBarApp folder of files directory and select '**New File**'. The next screen will prompt you to choose a temple for new file. Select **iOS → Source → Cocoa Touch Class**.

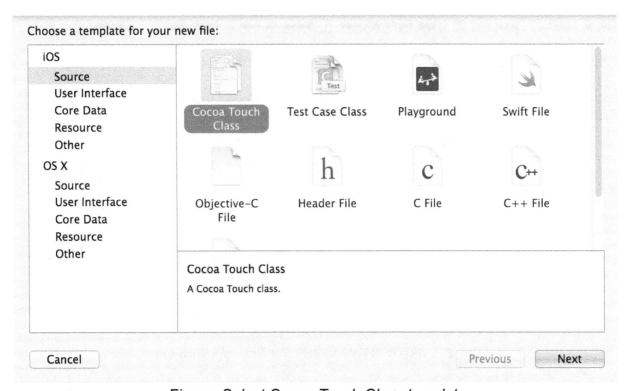

Figure: Select Cocoa Touch Class template

Click **Next**. The next screen let's you enter class name and parent class. Name the class '*ThirdViewController*'. Make sure it's a subclass of '*UIViewController*' and language is '*Swift*'.

Choose options for your new file:

Class: ThirdViewController

Subclass of: UIViewController

☐ Also create XIB file

iPhone

Language: Swift

Cancel   Previous   Next

Figure: Choose options for new class

Click **Next** and a new class file called *ThirdViewController.swift* will be generated.

Now to link *ThirdViewController* to the third view, do the following steps. Select ThirdView in the storyboard. Under 'Identity Inspector', select *ThirdViewController*.

Custom Class

Class   ThirdViewController

Module Current – TabBarApp

Identity

Storyboard ID

Restoration ID

☐ Use Storyboard ID

Figure: Link ThirdViewController file with third view

Once you have done this, we have connected ThirdViewController to the Third view.

Let's now add a button to the Third view and an action to that button to test that the connection is done properly. Zoom in all the way to the third view. Note that, if you want to drag and drop UI Controls onto a view in storyboard, you will need to zoom in all the way.

Drag a button into the third view and add the following simple action method in the *ThirdViewController.swift* file -

```
@IBAction func testButtonPressed(sender: AnyObject) {
    let alert = UIAlertController(title: "It works!", message: "Third view  alert",
preferredStyle: UIAlertControllerStyle.Alert)
    let action = UIAlertAction(title: "OK", style:  UIAlertActionStyle.Default, handler: nil)
    alert.addAction(action)
    presentViewController(alert, animated: true, completion: nil)
}
```

Next, connect the button in the Third view by control click drag from the button to the Third View Controller and select '*testButtonPressed*'.

Explanation

let alert = UIAlertController(title: "It works!", message: "Third view alert", preferredStyle: UIAlertControllerStyle.Alert)

The above line creates an *UIAlertController* instance and assigns that to the constant named *alert*. This will create an alert with the title 'It works!' and message 'Third view alert'.

let action = UIAlertAction(title: "OK", style: UIAlertActionStyle.Default, handler: nil)

The above line creates an *UIAlertAction* instance and assigns that to the constant named *action*. We create this *UIAlertAction* instance to add a button to the alert view. The title of the button is set to "OK".

alert.addAction(action)

The *addAction()* method of *UIAlertController* instance is used to add an action. We call this method to add the "OK" button to the alert view.

presentViewController(alert, animated: true, completion: nil)

Finally we call *presentViewController()* method to show the alert.

Running Your App

Now run the application in the simulator and observe that you have a tab bar application with three tab items. Clicking on each of the tabs brings a different view. Click on the third bar item and click on the button. An alert box will show.

Figure: Running the app

What You Have Learnt

You have learnt how to create a tab bar application using the storyboard feature of Xcode. You have learnt how to add additional tabs and link classes to them. Hence, what you have learned in other chapters can be integrated into tab bar applications e.g. Labels, SegmentedControl, WebView etc.

Chapter 8 - Creating TableViews

In this section, you will learn how to use a table view in a master detail based app.

In a master detail based app, you select items from a master table view and upon selecting an item, it brings you to a details page for that item. We will be displaying a list of friends in a table view and upon selecting one, we will be brought to the friends detail page of that friend.

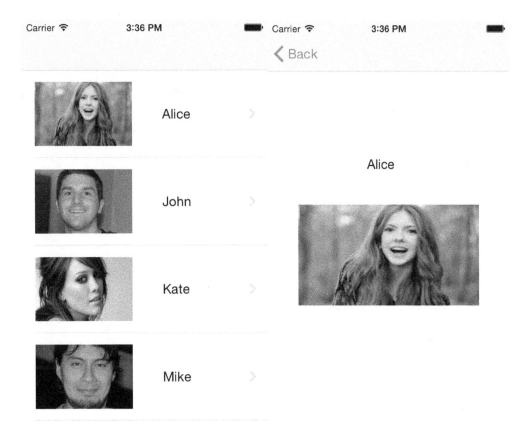

Figure: Running the completed app

Create a Single View Application for iPhone and name it 'FriendList'.

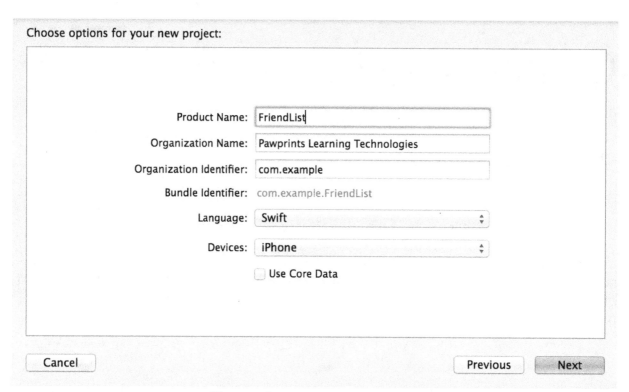

Choose options for your new project:

Product Name: FriendList

Organization Name: Pawprints Learning Technologies

Organization Identifier: com.example

Bundle Identifier: com.example.FriendList

Language: Swift

Devices: iPhone

Use Core Data

Cancel   Previous   Next

Figure: Create new application

Open the storyboard and disable size classes. Then select the default View Controller and delete it by pressing the delete key. We will learn how to build a table view controller manually from scratch, which will be better for our understanding.

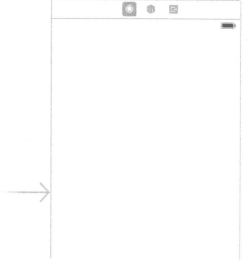

Figure: Select default view controller and delete it

Also delete the default ViewController.swift file.

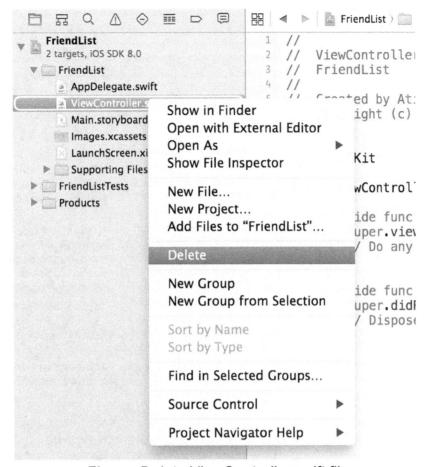

Figure: Delete ViewController.swift file

Next in the storyboard, drag a Table View Controller onto it.

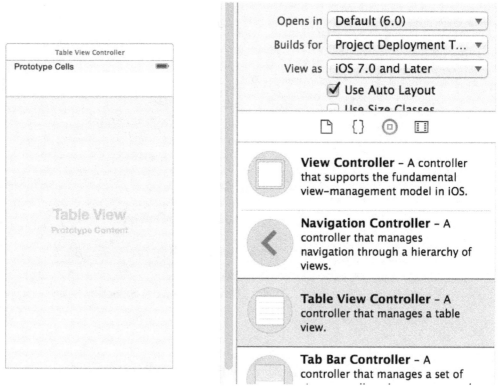

Figure: Add Table View Controller

In the project navigator, right click on the project and select '**New File...**'. The next screen will prompt you to choose a template. Select **iOS → Source → Cocoa Touch Class** and click **Next**.

The next screen will let you configure options for your new file. Enter '*FriendTableViewController*' as C**lass** name and make sure the value of **Subclass of** field is '*UITableViewController*'. From **Language** dropdown, select '*Swift*' as language.

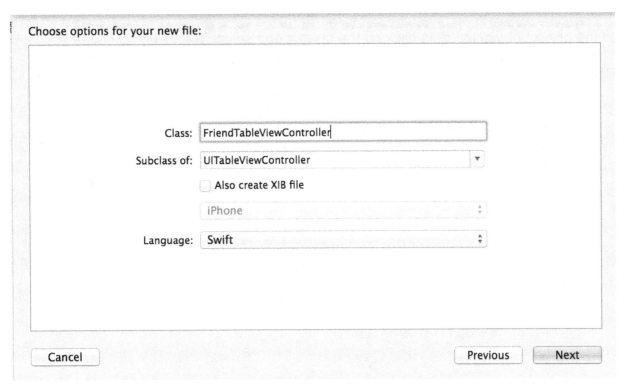

Figure: Create FriendTableViewController class

Click **Next** and a new file named *FriendTableViewController.swift* will be generated.

Now we need to link this newly generated class to table view controller. In the storyboard, select the table view controller and under identity inspector, select '*FriendTableViewController*'.

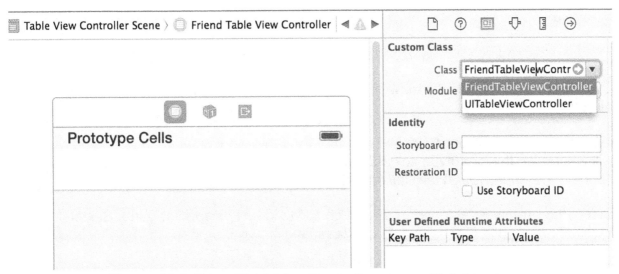

Figure: Link FriendTableViewController class with table view

Xcode allows us to create custom table view cells. We can easily design how it looks using the Xcode's interface builder tool. To do that, we first create a class for the table view cell.

In the project navigator, right click on the project and select '**New File...**'. The next screen will prompt you to choose a template. Select **iOS** → **Source** → **Cocoa Touch Class** and click **Next**.

The next screen will let you configure options for your new file. Enter '*FriendTableViewCell*' as **C**lass name and make sure the value of **Subclass of** field is '*UITableViewCell*'. From **Language** dropdown, select '*Swift*' as language.

Figure: Create class for table view cell

Click **Next**. The *FriendTableViewCell.swift* class file will be generated under project directory.

Next, go to the storyboard. You will see that the table view contains a prototype cell. We will customize this prototype cell according to our desired table view cell. But first let's connect the *FriendTableViewCell.swift* file with this prototype cell.

Select the prototype table view cell and go to the identity inspector pane. Select '*FriendTableViewCell*' as the value of **Class** field.

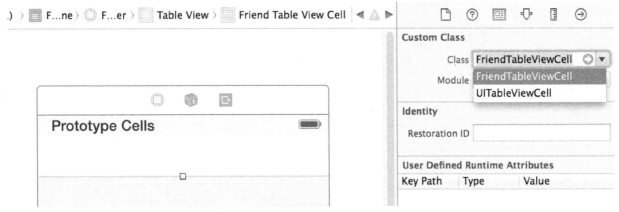

Figure: Link FriendTableViewCell with table view cell

Still selecting the table view cell, under attributes inspector, '**Identifier**' field, type '*FriendTableCell*'. We are going to identify the cell with the identifier '*FriendTableCell*'.

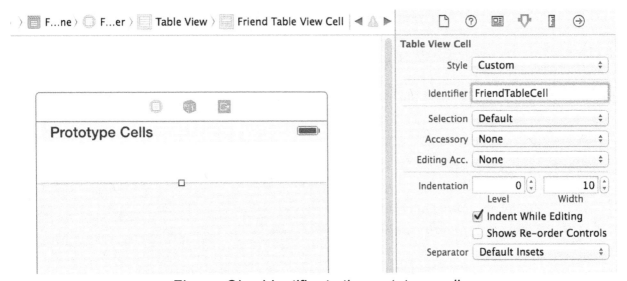

Figure: Give identifier to the prototype cell

Designing The TableViewCell

This is the interesting part. We can customize the look of our tableview cells! Just as how we can customize our views, we can do so in a similar fashion for our tableview cells.

Enlarge the cell by dragging it down. Next, drag an image view and a label in the cell.

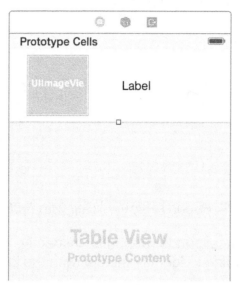

Figure: Designing the tableview cell

FriendTableViewCell.swift

In FriendTableViewCell.swift, fill in the below codes in bold.

import UIKit

class FriendTableViewCell: UITableViewCell {

    @IBOutlet var nameLabel: UILabel!
    @IBOutlet var friendImageView: UIImageView!

    override func awakeFromNib() {
    super.awakeFromNib()
    }

    override func setSelected(selected: Bool, animated: Bool) {
    super.setSelected(selected, animated: animated)
    }

}

We have just declared the outlets for the *imageview* and *label* of the tableview cell. Remember to connect the outlets with the corresponding UI controls. This time, let's do that in another way. Select the table view cell in your storyboard and go to *Connections Inspector* (the right most inspector). Under the **Outlets** section, you will see the two outlets (*friendImageView* and *nameLabel*) among other outlets.

Figure: Connections inspector

You can see the empty circle to the right of each connection type which indicates that they aren't connected to anything yet. If you put your mouse pointer within the circle, you will see that it changes to a plus icon. Put the mouse pointer within the circle next to *nameLabel,* click drag to label (don't press control button) and release it. As soon as you release the mouse button, the *nameLabel* outlet will be connected to the label control. In the same way, connect *friendImageView* outlet to the imageView.

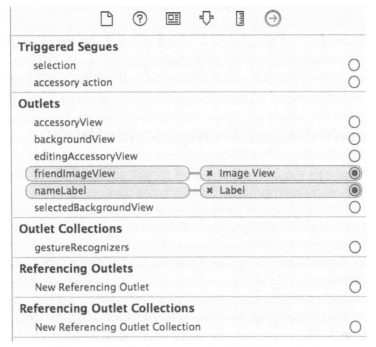

Figure: Outlets connected to UI controls

FriendTableViewController.swift

In *FriendTableViewController.swift* file, fill in the below codes. We will be storing the friend names and their corresponding image file names in two arrays.

```swift
import UIKit

class FriendTableViewController: UITableViewController {

    var images: [String] = []
    var names: [String] = []

    override func viewDidLoad() {
    super.viewDidLoad()

    images = ["alice.jpeg", "john.jpeg", "kate.jpeg", "mike.jpeg"]
    names = ["Alice", "John", "Kate", "Mike"]
    }

}
```

Here, we first declare two instance variables – *names* and *images*, both of them are arrays of String type. Initially we assign them an empty array (by specifying empty pair of brackets) because in swift, all instance variables must have a value. Within the viewDidLoad() method, we fill the *images* and *names* array with values. These arrays will be used to populate the table view. Now it's a good time to import the images. Check the assets folder for this chapter and you will see four images. You learned how to import images in a previous chapter. If you don't remember, feel free to check that again!

UITableViewController Delegate Methods

The following methods are the implementation of the UITableViewController delegate methods. That is, they require methods for the table view.

tableView(numberOfRowsInSection)

First, add in the below code to *FriendTableViewController.swift* file below the *viewDidLoad()* method -

```swift
override func tableView(tableView: UITableView, numberOfRowsInSection section: Int) -> Int {
    return names.count
}
```

The *tableView(numberOfRowsInSection)* method states how many rows to display in the table view. In this case, we will display the number of elements that are in our array. That is often the case when we use tableviews.

The *count* property of *names* array returns the number of elements in the array.

tableView(cellForRowAtIndexPath)

This delegate method presents the content to be displayed for each row of the table view, i.e. the tableview cell. Add the below code in your *FriendTableViewController.swift* file -

```
override func tableView(tableView: UITableView, cellForRowAtIndexPath indexPath:
NSIndexPath) -> UITableViewCell {
let cell = tableView.dequeueReusableCellWithIdentifier("FriendTableCell")  as
FriendTableViewCell
    cell.nameLabel.text = names[indexPath.row]
    cell.friendImageView.image = UIImage(named: images[indexPath.row])
    return cell
}
```

Explanation of Code

let cell = tableView.dequeueReusableCellWithIdentifier("FriendTableCell") as
FriendTableViewCell

In the above code, we use the *dequeReusableCellWithIdentifier()* method of *tableView* to check if there are any reusable cells to be used with the identifier "FriendTableCell". If there is, we reuse the cells. It is a good idea to reuse cells which is more efficient than creating new cells all the time. You might be wondering how do we get reusable cells because we haven't created any cells yet. If you remember, we have a prototype table view cell which we designed a while ago and we set a identifier for that cell. When we call the *dequeReusableCellWithIdentifier()* method, if it doesn't find any reusable cell, it will create a new cell using the prototype cell from storyboard. We then typecast the table view cell to our custom *FriendTableViewCell* class using the **'as'** keyword. The tableview cell is assigned to the variable named **cell**.

cell.nameLabel.text = names[indexPath.row]

Next, we assign the *nameLabel* in each cell as the string value obtained from the *names* array. Each row retrieves the element at *indexPath.row* index of *names* array.

cell.friendImageView.image = UIImage(named: images[indexPath.row])

We then retrieve and populate the image for each cell in a similar fashion as the name except that we have to create a UIImage object from the given image file name and assign the image to the cell's *friendImageView* property.

return cell

Finally we need to return the tableview cell.

Running the App

Run the project. You should see a tableview of cells which consists of a populated image and label each.

Figure: Running the app

We will next extend the tableview such that when we click on each individual cell, it brings us to a detail page.

Creating A Details View

In the storyboard, drag a new View Controller into the canvas. This View Controller will be our friends details view controller.

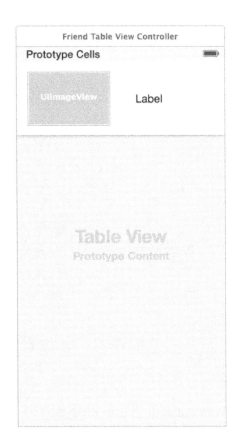

Figure: Add a new view controller

Next, we will create a class for that new view controller.

In the project navigator, right click on the project and select '**New File...**'. The next screen will prompt you to choose a template. Select **iOS → Source → Cocoa Touch Class** and click **Next**.

The next screen will let you configure options for your new file. Enter '*FriendDetailViewController*' as C**lass** name and make sure the value of **Subclass of** field is '*UIViewController*'. From **Language** dropdown, select '*Swift*' as language.

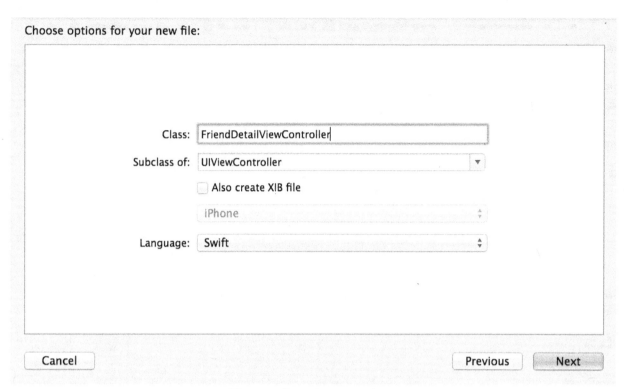

Figure: Create new class

Now, let's set this new class as the class for details view controller. From storyboard, select the details view controller. Under identity inspector, select '*FriendDetailViewController*' in the *class* field.

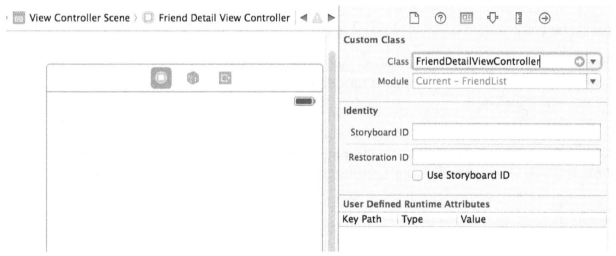

Figure: Set class for detail view controller

Embedding the Navigation Controller

We will next embed a navigation controller into our project. You do this by first selecting the table view, then go to **Editor** → **Embed In** → **Navigation Controller**. A navigation controller will then appear on the left of the table view.

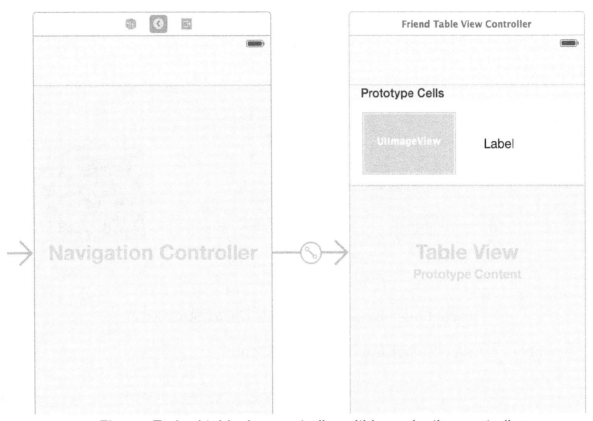

Figure: Embed tableview controller within navigation controller

With a navigation controller, our views act like a stack where views are placed on top of one another. The default view on the navigation controller is the table view. When we click on one cell of the table view, we push a detailed view onto the stack. When we click on the back button of the detailed view, we pop the view off the stack and thus show the underlying table view.

Next, drag control click from the table view cell to the new view. Select 'push' under *Selection Segue*. As previously mentioned, we select 'push' as the navigation controller acts like a stack where we push and pop views on and off the stack.

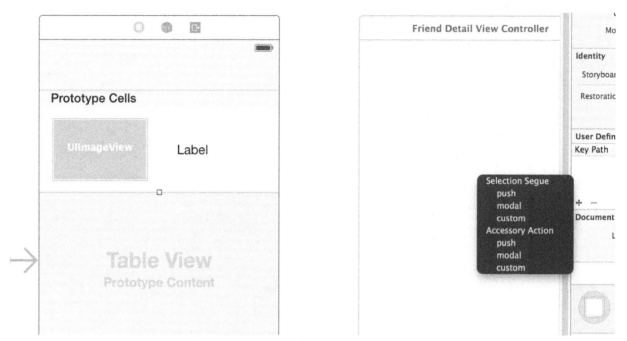

Figure: Creating segue from table cell to detail view

Your storyboard should now look like the following figure -

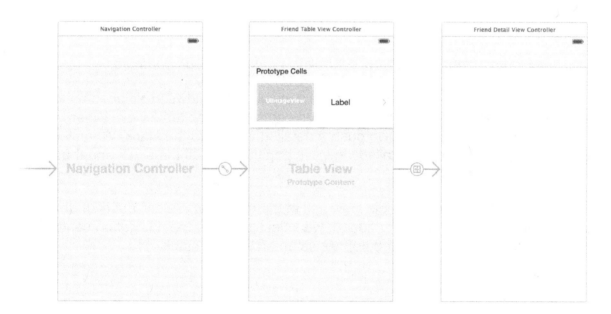

Figure: Storyboard with views

In the new view, drag a label and image view into the view -

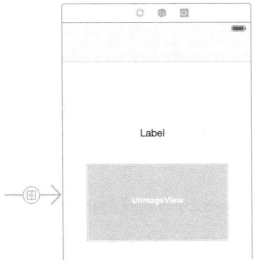

Figure: Add label and image view

FriendDetailViewController.swift

Update FriendDetailViewController.swift file with the following code -

import UIKit

class FriendDetailViewController: UIViewController {

  @IBOutlet weak var nameLabel: UILabel!
  @IBOutlet weak var imageView: UIImageView!

  var friendName: String!
  var friendImageFileName: String!

  override func viewDidLoad() {
    super.viewDidLoad()

    nameLabel.text = friendName
    imageView.image = UIImage(named: friendImageFileName)
  }

}

Explanation

@IBOutlet weak var nameLabel: UILabel!
@IBOutlet weak var imageView: UIImageView!

We declare two Outlets, one for the label and another one for the image view.

var friendName: String!
var friendImageFileName: String!

Next, we declare two instance variables of String type. The variable named *friendName* will store the value of name of the friend and the variable *friendImageFileName* will store the value of the image file name of the friend. The values of these two variables will be set from *FriendTableViewController*. Finally within *viewDidLoad* method, we use the above two instance variables to set the text value of label and image of the imageView.

nameLabel.text = friendName
imageView.image = UIImage(named: friendImageFileName)

Now connect the label and image view to the Outlets.

Passing Values From The TableView to the Detailed View

Passing values from the master table view to the detailed view is similar to the way we pass values from one view to another using the 'prepareForSegue' method. You can refer to the chapter on Switching views for a more in-depth explanation on 'prepareForSegue'.

First, we identify the segue from the table view to the detailed view by selecting it in the storyboard. Under the attributes inspector, identifier field, type in 'ShowFriendDetail'.

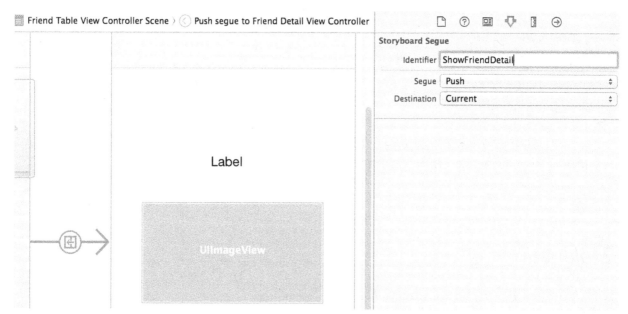

Figure: Set identifier for the segue

FriendTableViewController.swift

Now in *FriendTableViewController.swift*, add the below method -

```
override func prepareForSegue(segue: UIStoryboardSegue, sender: AnyObject?) {
    if segue.identifier == "ShowFriendDetail" {
        let controller = segue.destinationViewController as FriendDetailViewController
        let indexPath = tableView.indexPathForCell(sender as FriendTableViewCell)
        controller.friendName = names[indexPath!.row]
        controller.friendImageFileName = images[indexPath!.row]
    }
}
```

Explanation of Code

if segue.identifier == "ShowFriendDetail" {

We first check if the segue's identifier is 'ShowFriendDetail'.

let controller = segue.destinationViewController as FriendDetailViewController

If it is, we use the *destinationViewController* property of *segue* object to get the view controller which will appear next - in our case, it is *FriendDetailViewController*.

let indexPath = tableView.indexPathForCell(sender as FriendTableViewCell)

In the above line, we get the indexPath of the table row selected by the user.

controller.friendName = names[indexPath!.row]
 controller.friendImageFileName = images[indexPath!.row]

These two lines set the values of *friendName* and *friendImageFileName* instance variables of *FriendDetailViewController*. The *row* property of *indexPath* returns the selected table view row. Using that row index, we get the friend's name and image file name from the corresponding arrays. Thus when we go to the detail view, the detail view can retrieve these values and display on its label and image view.

Running the App

Run the app now. Upon selecting one of the table cells, you will be brought to the detail view showing the name and image of that friend.

Congratulations! You have learned how to use a table view as well as implement your own custom table view cells.

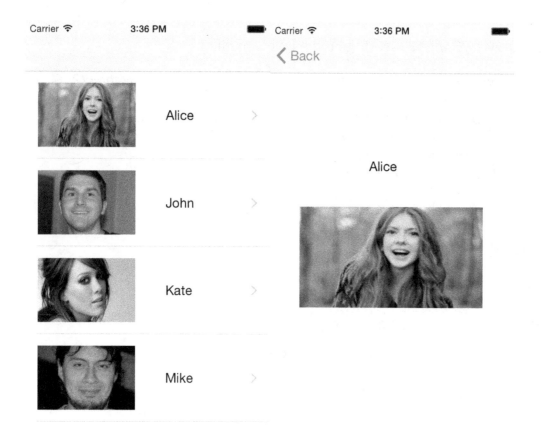

Figure: Running the app

Chapter 9 - Detecting Touches and Taps

In this chapter, you will create an app that detects touches and taps. Although there is a simpler way to do it using Gesture Recognizers which we will elaborate in the next chapter, it is useful to understand how to detect Touches and Taps using delegates to increase our understanding about them.

Create a Single View iPhone application and name it *TouchTapApp*. Select the storyboard and disable size classes. Now drag three labels into the view.

Figure: Add three labels into the view

Click on the View itself and go to the Attributes inspector.

Click on the checkboxes 'User Interaction Enabled' and 'Multiple Touch'.

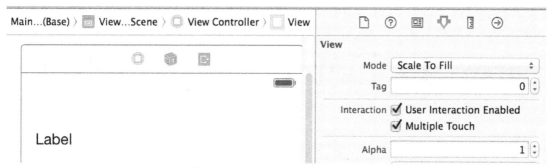

Figure: Enable interaction attributes

Create the Outlets for the labels with the below code in *ViewController.swift* file. These labels will show the number of taps and touches.

import UIKit

```
class ViewController: UIViewController {
  @IBOutlet weak var messageLabel: UILabel!
  @IBOutlet weak var tapsLabel: UILabel!
  @IBOutlet weak var touchesLabel: UILabel!
}
```

Connect the Outlets to the labels in the view.

Next, fill in the below codes in *ViewController.swift* immediately below the Outlets declaration -

```
override func touchesBegan(touches: NSSet, withEvent event: UIEvent) {
  messageLabel.text = "Touches Began"
  updateLabels(touches)
}

override func touchesCancelled(touches: NSSet!, withEvent event: UIEvent!) {
  messageLabel.text = "Touches Cancelled"
  updateLabels(touches)
}

override func touchesEnded(touches: NSSet, withEvent event: UIEvent) {
  messageLabel.text = "Touches Stopped"
  updateLabels(touches)
}

override func touchesMoved(touches: NSSet, withEvent event: UIEvent) {
  messageLabel.text = "Drag Detected"
  updateLabels(touches)
}
```

Xcode will throw a bunch of errors because we have referenced a function name that we have not declared yet. That's fine, we will fix that soon.

Explanation

There are four methods called regarding touches. When a touch first happens, the *touchesBegan* method is called. When a touch ends, i.e. finger is lifted, the *touchesEnd* method is called. When there is a touch-drag, the *touchesMoved* method is called. When a touch is cancelled, the method *touchesCancelled* is called.

The updateLabels method

We next implement the *updateLabels* method in *ViewController.swift* file -

```
func updateLabels(touches: NSSet) {
    var numTaps = touches.anyObject()?.tapCount
    tapsLabel.text = "\(numTaps!) taps detected"

    var numTouches = touches.count
    touchesLabel.text = "\(numTouches) touches detected"
}
```

Explanation

The *updateLabels* method is called by the touch methods which detect touches. This method retrieves the tap count and touch count from the *touches* object.

```
var numTaps = touches.anyObject()?.tapCount
tapsLabel.text = "\(numTaps!) taps detected"
```

We first retrieve the number of times the view is tapped using the *tapCount* property and we then show that to the label.

```
var numTouches = touches.count
touchesLabel.text = "\(numTouches) touches detected"
```

The *count* property of *touches* object returns the number of current touches there are on the view.

Run and deploy your project to a device (on how to deploy your project to a device, see Deploying your apps to a device chapter in Appendix A). Try tapping and touching with multiple fingers and note the label messages.

Summary

You have learnt how to detect taps and touches on a view!

Chapter 10 - Detecting Gestures

In this section, you will create an app that can detect taps, pinches, swipes, pan, rotation and more! What's more, you do not have to write code to detect any of the gestures! This is made possible by Gesture Recognizers available in Xcode interface builder.

Create a Single View application and name it GestureApp. Drag a *webview* into the view. Declare an Outlet for the *webview* by adding the code in bold below the *ViewController.swift* file -

import UIKit

class ViewController: UIViewController {
    @IBOutlet weak var **webView: UIWebView!**

    override func viewDidLoad() {
    super.viewDidLoad()
    }

}

Next, connect the Outlet by drag clicking from View Controller in the storyboard to the *webview*.

We will next learn how to detect swipes on a view. Drag and drop a *Swipe Gesture Recognizer* into the view. When you do so, the recognizer will be added to the bar above the view. Drag another *Swipe Gesture Recognizer* into the view.

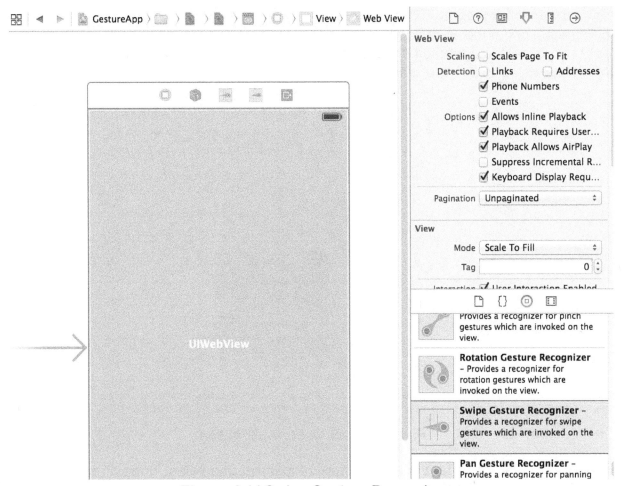

Figure: Add Swipe Gesture Recognizer

Click on the left gesture recognizer in the bar and under the attributes inspector, chose '*Left*' in the **Swipe** field. Notice that, there are also 'Right', 'Up', and 'Down' swipe options available. This gesture recognizer will be used to detect left swipes.

Figure: Select Left swipe

Next, control click drag from the left gesture recognizer to the web view. Select 'goForward' under the *Sent Actions*. You have just connected a left swipe gesture to the 'goForward' delegate method of the webview. So when we use the webview to browse Internet sites, to go forward, swipe left!

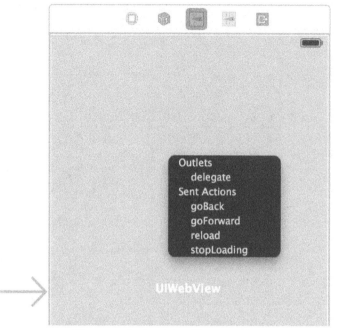

Figure: Select 'goForward' action

Repeat the same steps for the right gesture recognizer and select 'goBack' when you drag control click to the *webview*.

Finally, add the below codes in bold to the viewDidLoad to set the *webview* to a website when the app starts up.

```
override func viewDidLoad() {
    super.viewDidLoad()

    var url = NSURL.URLWithString("http://www.apple.com")
    var request = NSURLRequest(URL: url)
    webView.loadRequest(request)
}
```

Run the app on an actual device if possible. Otherwise try it with the simulator. Browse through a couple of pages in the Apple website. Try swiping left and right. What happens? You can go back to previous/next page by swiping! Isn't it wonderful?

Linking Gestures to Actions

You can also link gestures to actions. In this section, I will show you how to link a pinch gesture to an action. The process is same for other gesture types.

Add the below action method to ViewController.swift file -

```
@IBAction func pinch(sender: AnyObject) {
    var alert = UIAlertController(title: "Pinch", message: nil, preferredStyle: .Alert)
    alert.addAction(UIAlertAction(title: "OK", style: .Default, handler: nil))
    presentViewController(alert, animated: true, completion: nil)
}
```

The above action method should look very familiar to you. It just shows an alert message. You have written code to show alert several times by now.

Next go to storyboard and drag a 'Pinch Gesture Recognizer' from object library to your view. Like the swipe gesture recognizer, the pinch gesture recognizer will be added to the top bar.

Link the pinch gesture recognizer to the action method by control clicking from the pinch gesture recognizer to the View Controller and select the action 'pinch'.

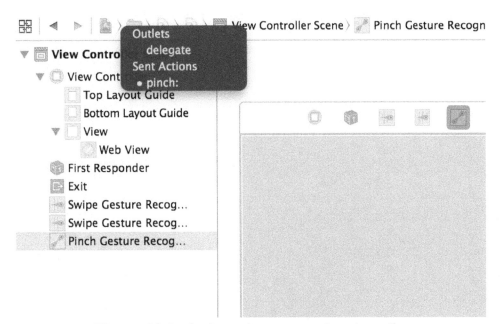

Figure: Link pinch gesture recognizer to action

Running the App

Upon running the app, try pinching the screen. You should see an alert message which is triggered by the pinch gesture. With this, you can create more complex actions to complement with a specific gesture. Other gestures like rotate, pan and more all work the same way. Try it!

Chapter 11 - Building Location Based Apps

In this chapter, you will build an application that makes use of the Map and GPS capabilities of the device.

First, create a new iPhone Single View Application and name it *LocationBasedApp*. Next, select the *Main.storyboard* file and disable size classes.

From project navigator, select the project directory and go to **Build Phases > Link Binary With Libraries** and click the **+** button to add new framework. From the popup, select *MapKit.framework* and click **Add**.

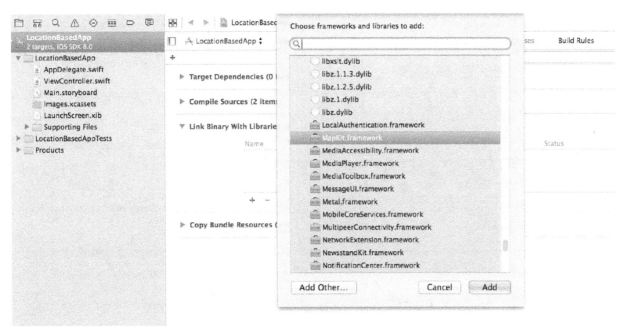

Figure: Add MapKit framework to project

This will add the MapKit framework to your project.

In the storyboard, drag a *MapKit View* and a button into the view.

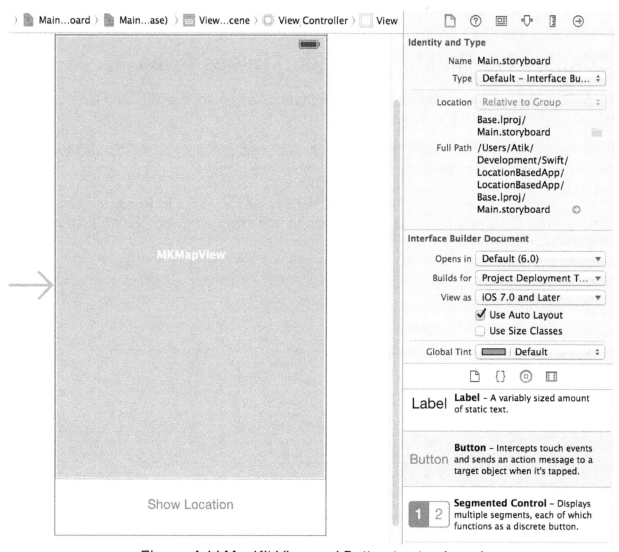

Identity and Type

Name Main.storyboard

Type Default – Interface Bu... ⇕

Location Relative to Group ⇕

Base.lproj/
Main.storyboard

Full Path /Users/Atik/
Development/Swift/
LocationBasedApp/
LocationBasedApp/
Base.lproj/
Main.storyboard ⊙

Interface Builder Document

Opens in Default (6.0) ▼

Builds for Project Deployment T... ▼

View as iOS 7.0 and Later ▼

☑ Use Auto Layout

☐ Use Size Classes

Global Tint ▭ | Default ⇕

Label **Label** – A variably sized amount of static text.

Button **Button** – Intercepts touch events and sends an action message to a target object when it's tapped.

1 2 **Segmented Control** – Displays multiple segments, each of which functions as a discrete button.

MKMapView

Show Location

Figure: Add MapKit View and Button to storyboard

Add the statements in bold to your ViewController.swift file -

import UIKit
import MapKit

class ViewController: UIViewController {

  @IBOutlet weak var mapView: MKMapView!

  @IBAction func showLocation(sender: AnyObject) {

  }

  override func viewDidLoad() {
    super.viewDidLoad()
  }

}

Explanation

import MapKit

This line imports the *MapKit* framework. The *MapKit View* and all the map related functionalities come from this *MapKit* framework.

@IBOutlet weak var mapView: MKMapView!

We declare an outlet for the *MapKit View*. Be sure to connect the outlet with with the *MapKit View* in thestoryboard.

  @IBAction func showLocation(sender: AnyObject) {

  }

We next declare an action. Connect this action with the button in the storyboard.

At this point, if you run the app, you will have a working app that shows your current location! If you are running from the simulator, the location will probably be showing Apple's headquarters. If you deploy to a device, it will show your actual location!

Show Location

Figure: The app showing map of your location

Now let's further improve our app. Add the CoreLocation framework to your project.

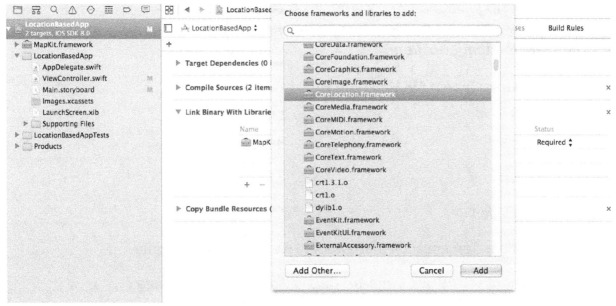

Figure: Add CoreLocation framework

Next, add the codes in bold into *ViewController.swift* file -

import UIKit
import MapKit
import CoreLocation

*class ViewController: UIViewController, **CLLocationManagerDelegate** {*

  @IBOutlet weak var mapView: MKMapView!

  var lm: CLLocationManager = CLLocationManager()

  @IBAction func showLocation(sender: AnyObject) {

  }

  override func viewDidLoad() {
    super.viewDidLoad()

    let authStatus: CLAuthorizationStatus =
CLLocationManager.authorizationStatus()

    if authStatus == .NotDetermined {
      lm.requestWhenInUseAuthorization()
      return
    }

    lm.delegate = self

```
lm.desiredAccuracy = kCLLocationAccuracyBest
lm.distanceFilter = kCLDistanceFilterNone
lm.startUpdatingLocation()

    mapView.mapType = MKMapType.Hybrid
  }

}
```

Explanation

import CoreLocation

We first import the *CoreLocation* framework to work with location data.

class ViewController: UIViewController, CLLocationManagerDelegate {

We want our *ViewController* class to be notified when the device's location is updated. So we declare *ViewController* as *CLLocationManagerDelegate*.

var lm: CLLocationManager = CLLocationManager()

We create a new instance of *CLLocationManager* class. This *CLLocationManager* class instance will be used to deal with location data.

let authStatus: CLAuthorizationStatus = CLLocationManager.authorizationStatus()

```
    if authStatus == .NotDetermined {
        lm.requestWhenInUseAuthorization()
        return
    }
```

We need the user's permission to access his location data. This is new as of iOS 8. This permission is asked only once. Just adding these above lines isn't enough for asking permission. We also need to add a special key to the app's *Info.plist* file.

Open the Info.plist file and right click somewhere inside Info.plist and choose **Add Row**. For the key, type **NSLocationWhenInUseUsageDescription i**n the value column, type "*This app requires GPS coordinates of your location.*"

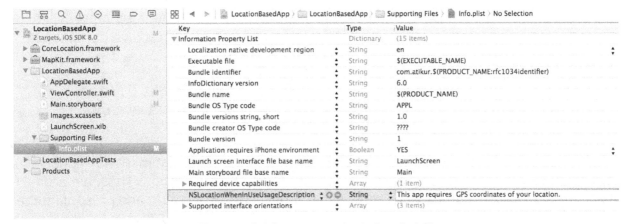

Figure: Add new row to Info.plist file

lm.delegate = self
lm.desiredAccuracy = kCLLocationAccuracyBest

With the LocationManager, you can set the desired accuracy of the positioning. Do note that the higher the accuracy, the more time and battery power is needed to pinpoint the exact location.

lm.distanceFilter = kCLDistanceFilterNone

You can also set distance filter which is the distance the device must move before an update in position occurs.

lm.startUpdatingLocation()

Finally, you start the location update.

mapView.mapType = MKMapType.Hybrid

This determines the map type. We set it as hybrid type here, but you can also choose Satelite or Standard as well.

locationManager(didUpdateToLocation: fromLocation:) method

Next, add the following method to *ViewController.swift* file -

```
func locationManager(manager: CLLocationManager!, didUpdateToLocation
newLocation: CLLocation!, fromLocation oldLocation: CLLocation!) {
    var span = MKCoordinateSpan(latitudeDelta: 0.001, longitudeDelta:  0.001)
    var region = MKCoordinateRegion(center: newLocation.coordinate, span:  span)
    mapView.setRegion(region, animated: true)
}
```

Explanation

The *locationManager(didUpdateToLocation: fromLocation:)* delegate method is called when an update in location occurs. With this delegate method, we receive both the old and the current new location.

var span = MKCoordinateSpan(latitudeDelta: 0.001, longitudeDelta: 0.001)
var region = MKCoordinateRegion(center: newLocation.coordinate, span: span)
mapView.setRegion(region, animated: true)

With the above codes, we get our new current location with the argument *newLocation* and set the map's region with zoom span of 0.001 to the new location. Thus, we are effectively constantly updating our map with our new current location and presenting the zoom level.

Running the App

When you run the app, you will see that it asks for accessing location permission.

Figure: App asking for location permission

This permission will be asked only once. Go ahead and click **Allow**. You will next see the hybrid map zooming into your location as specified by the span property. This is better than just showing a global map and having to spend time zooming in.

Show Location

Figure: Showing hybrid map

Displaying Annotations In Maps

We will further improve the app by having a pin on our location. The pin is called an 'Annotation'.

Add the following instance variable to *ViewController.swift* file, right below where you declared *CLLocationManager* instance -

var annotation: MKPointAnnotation = MKPointAnnotation()

Also add the following code within *locationManager(didUpdateToLocation: fromLocation:)* method, below the line where you set map region -

annotation.title = "I am here!"
annotation.coordinate = newLocation.coordinate
mapView.showAnnotations([annotation], animated: true)

If you run the app now, the map will show a pin at your location. If you click the pin, it will show the text 'I am here!' in a bubble.

Show Location

Figure: Showing annotation to the map

Explanation

var annotation: MKPointAnnotation = MKPointAnnotation()

The above line declares an *MKPointAnnotation* class instance and assigns that to the variable *annotation*. We declared *annotation* as an instance variable of *ViewController* class, because we need to access that from several methods.

annotation.title = "I am here!"

We set the *title* attribute of *annotation* as "I am here!". This is the text shown in a bubble when you click the pin on the map.

annotation.coordinate = newLocation.coordinate

The *coordinate* attribute of *annotation* determines where the annotation should appear. We set that to the *newLocation*, which is the updated location of the user.

mapView.showAnnotations([annotation], animated: true)

Finally, we show the annotation in the map.

Reverse Geo-Coding

We shall further improve our location based app to reverse geo-code the GPS coordinates to return us the actual address.

Open ViewController.swift file and add two more instance variables -

var geocoder = CLGeocoder()
var location: CLLocation?

The first variable creates an instance of the *CLGeocoder* class and stores the reference in the variable *geocoder*. This will be used for reverse geo-coding. The *location* variable will hold the latest location of the user. This variable is defined as an optional, because *location* might not be available all the time. (the location fix from a device requires some time - moreover, your device might have a weak GPS signal or cell tower signal. Some devices like iPods or devices which use wifi connection data to obtain location information do not have GPS).

Next, add the following line of code within the *locationManager(didUpdateToLocation: fromLocation:)* method, below the line where you set annotation -

location = newLocation

As you can see, you are updating the *location* variable with the new location obtained.

Finally, update the *showLocation()* action with following code -

```
@IBAction func showLocation(sender: AnyObject) {
    if let location = location {
        geocoder.reverseGeocodeLocation(location, completionHandler: {
            placemarks, error in
            if error == nil && !placemarks.isEmpty {
                var placemark = placemarks.last as CLPlacemark
                var locationString = "\(placemark.locality) \(placemark.postalCode), \
(placemark.country)"
                self.annotation.subtitle = locationString
            }
        })
    }
}
```

Explanation

We first check if the *location* variable has any value -

119

```
if let location = location {
```

Remember that the *location* variable is 'optional?' This means that the *location* variable can have either any valid *CLLocation* type data or it could be *nil*. The above syntax is used to unwrap the optional value. As a result, if the *location* instance variable holds a valid *CLLocation* data, then that will be assigned to another variable (which is named *location* as well) and the code inside the *if block* will be executed. Though it may seem confusing, you will see this a lot throughout your iOS development career with Swift.

```
geocoder.reverseGeocodeLocation(location, completionHandler: {
    placemarks, error in
    if error == nil && !placemarks.isEmpty {
        var placemark = placemarks.last as CLPlacemark
        var locationString = "\(placemark.locality) \(placemark.postalCode), \
(placemark.country)"
        self.annotation.subtitle = locationString
    }
})
```

The above piece of code performs the reverse geo-code operation and gets the address of *location* variable's coordinates. The location variable is passed to the reverseGeocodeLocation() method as the first parameter. The second parameter is a closure (which is a block of code) which runs after the reverseGeocodeLocation() method returns. Closures are like functions, but without any name (some programming language refer it as anonymous functions). Like functions, closures can take parameters. In our case, there are two parameters *placemarks* and *error*. We can not simply assume that the geo-coder returns a valid address. Sometimes it might fail (because of no recognized address at the user's current location or that a data connection isn't available). We check for this in the following code -

```
if error == nil && !placemarks.isEmpty {
```

In case we have a valid response from the geo-coder, the *placemarks* parameter will be an array which may contain more than one address. For us, we simply take the last one -

```
var placemark = placemarks.last as CLPlacemark
```

Next, we extract info from *placemark* to construct the address -

```
var locationString = "\(placemark.locality) \(placemark.postalCode), \
(placemark.country)"
```

Finally, we set the address to the annotation variable's *subtitle* property -

```
self.annotation.subtitle = locationString
```

Notice the *self* keyword before the annotation instance variable. While you can access instance variables with the self keyword from methods, its not strictly required. But from within a closure, you are strictly required to use the *self* keyword before instance variables.

Running the App

Run the app and click the 'Show Location' button. If you click the annotation pin now, you will see that the reverse geo-coded address shows up.

Show Location

Figure: Running finished app

Chapter 12 - Taking Photos and Accessing Photo Library

In this chapter, we will create an app that can retrieve photos from the photo library of your iOS device and show it on an *imageview*. Additionally, the app can take photos with the camera and show the image taken on the *imageview* as well.

Use Camera

Access Photo Library

Figure: Running the app

Getting Started

Create a new iPhone Single View application and name it as PhotoGrabber. In the storyboard, drag an ImageView and two buttons. Change the labels of the buttons as "Use Camera" and "Access Photo Library".

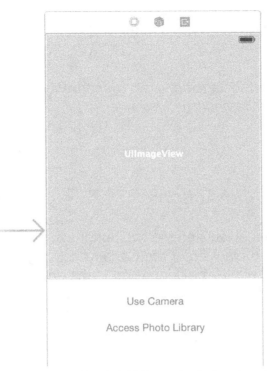

Figure: Add UI controls to view

Open the ViewController.swift file and replace its content with the following code -

import UIKit

class ViewController: UIViewController, UIImagePickerControllerDelegate, UINavigationControllerDelegate {

  @IBOutlet weak var imageView: UIImageView!

  @IBAction func choosePhotoFromLibrary(sender: AnyObject) {
    let imagePicker = UIImagePickerController()
    imagePicker.sourceType = .PhotoLibrary
    imagePicker.delegate = self
    presentViewController(imagePicker, animated: true, completion: nil)
  }

  @IBAction func takePhotoFromCamera(sender: AnyObject) {
    let imagePicker = UIImagePickerController()
    imagePicker.sourceType = .Camera
    imagePicker.delegate = self
    presentViewController(imagePicker, animated: true, completion: nil)
  }

  func imagePickerController(picker: UIImagePickerController!, didFinishPickingImage image: UIImage!, editingInfo: [NSObject : AnyObject]!) {

```
        imageView.image = image
        dismissViewControllerAnimated(true, completion: nil)
    }

    func imagePickerControllerDidCancel(picker: UIImagePickerController) {
        dismissViewControllerAnimated(true, completion: nil)
    }

}
```

Connecting Outlets and Actions

Connect the outlet to the *imageview* and the two buttons to the *choosePhotoFromLibrary* and *takePhotoFromCamera* actions. As you can guess, the button labeled 'Use Camera' should be connected to the action *takePhotoFromCamera* while the other button should be connected to the *choosePhotoFromLibrary* action.

Explanation of Code

class ViewController: UIViewController, UIImagePickerControllerDelegate, UINavigationControllerDelegate

As you can see, the *ViewController* class conforms both *UIImagePickerControllerDelegate* and *UINavigationControllerDelegate*.

```
    @IBAction func choosePhotoFromLibrary(sender: AnyObject) {
        let imagePicker = UIImagePickerController()
        imagePicker.sourceType = .PhotoLibrary
        imagePicker.delegate = self
        presentViewController(imagePicker, animated: true, completion: nil)
    }
```

The *choosePhotoFromLibrary* action is called when a user clicks the 'Access Photo Library' button. Within this action method, we first create an instance of a *UIImagePickerController* instance. The *UIImagePickerController* is a view controller except that it comes with *UIKit*. This view controller takes care of the entire process of taking new photos and picking them from the user's photo library.

As you can see, after we create the UIImagePickerController instance, all we need to do is to configure the picker, set its delegate and present it. We set the *ViewController* class as the delegate of *UIImagePickerController*. When the user closes the image picker screen, the delegate methods will be called and it handles the rest. We will examine them in a moment.

Take a look at the following line -

imagePicker.sourceType = .PhotoLibrary

The *sourceType* of picker is set to *PhotoLibrary*, which means that picker will let the user pick an image from the photo library of a iOS device.

If you take a look at the other action method, *takePhotoFromCamera*, you will see that, the code is exactly the same except the difference in *sourceType* of picker -

```
@IBAction func takePhotoFromCamera(sender: AnyObject) {
    let imagePicker = UIImagePickerController()
    imagePicker.sourceType = .Camera
    imagePicker.delegate = self
    presentViewController(imagePicker, animated: true, completion: nil)
}
```

Since the *takePhotoFromCamera* method will handle taking images using the device's camera, the sourceType of picker is set to *Camera*.

Next, we add two delegate methods.

```
func imagePickerControllerDidCancel(picker: UIImagePickerController) {
    dismissViewControllerAnimated(true, completion: nil)
}
```

This delegate method is called when user cancels the image picking operation. We simply dismiss the image picker view controller.

```
func imagePickerController(picker: UIImagePickerController!, didFinishPickingImage image: UIImage!, editingInfo: [NSObject : AnyObject]!) {
    imageView.image = image
    dismissViewControllerAnimated(true, completion: nil)
}
```

This delegate method is called when a user selects an image from the photo library (or captured image taken through camera). The image selected (or taken through camera) is passed as a method argument. We set that image to the *imageview*. We then dismiss the image picker controller.

Running the App

Within the simulator, you obviously cannot test the camera functionality. For that, you will need a real iOS device with camera. If you have a real iOS device, deploy the application on to your device (Appendix A). Otherwise, if you run the application on the simulator, you can only test the feature of picking image from photo library. If you click the 'Use Camera' button, the app will crash in the simulator.

Whatever the case, either take a photo with your device's camera, or just click the "Access Photo Library" button while running the app on simulator. After you select a photo (or take one through your device's camera), the photo will be shown in the *imageview*.

Use Camera

Access Photo Library

Figure: Running Application

Chapter 13 - Accessing the Address Book

We will be creating an app that accesses the phone's address book and display the contact's image (if any) and his/her first name.

Getting Started

Create a new Single View iPhone application and name it as *AddressBook*.

Click **AddressBook** from project navigator and select the tab **Build Phases**. Under the section titled **Link Binary with Libraries**, click the '**+**'. You will see a prompt to choose frameworks and libraries to add -

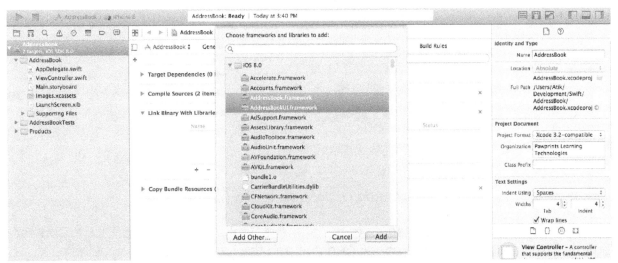

Figure: Add frameworks to project

Select both the *AddressBook.framework* and *AddressBookUI.framework* and click **Add**. Both these frameworks will be linked to your project.

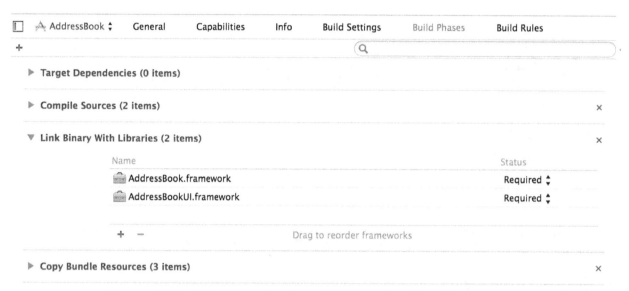

Name	Status
AddressBook.framework	Required ⇕
AddressBookUI.framework	Required ⇕

Figure: Linked AddressBook and AddressBookUI frameworks

Next, drag a UIImageView, a UILabel and a button into the storyboard view. Rename the button label as 'Pick a Contact' and UILabel text to 'Contact Name'.

Figure: Add UI controls to storyboard

We will let the user pick a contact from the address book by clicking the 'Pick a Contact' button. The label will show the contact's name and the *imageview* will show the contact's image (if available).

Open the *ViewController.swift* file and declare two outlets for the name label and *imageview* -

@IBOutlet weak var photo: UIImageView!
@IBOutlet weak var nameLabel: UILabel!

Don't forget to connect the outlets to the *imageview* and label.

Next, add the following action to *ViewController.swift* file, which will allow the user to select a contact from the address book -

```
@IBAction func selectContact(sender: AnyObject) {
    var picker = ABPeoplePickerNavigationController()
    picker.peoplePickerDelegate = self
    presentViewController(picker, animated: true, completion: nil)
}
```

Connect the button to the *selectContact* action.

Explanation of Code

var picker = ABPeoplePickerNavigationController()

This line creates a new *ABPeoplePickerNavigationController* instance and assigns that to the variable named *picker*.

picker.peoplePickerDelegate = self

We then set the *ViewController* class as the delegate of people picker navigation controller.

presentViewController(picker, animated: true, completion: nil)

Finally, we present the people picker navigation controller view.

Adding Delegates

Open the *ViewController.swift* file and modify the *ViewController* class declaration line to conform *ABPeoplePickerNavigationControllerDelegate*.

```
class ViewController: UIViewController, ABPeoplePickerNavigationControllerDelegate {
```

Next, add the following delegate method to the *ViewController* class -

```
func peoplePickerNavigationController(peoplePicker:
ABPeoplePickerNavigationController!, didSelectPerson person: ABRecord!) {
    var contactName = ABRecordCopyValue(person,
kABPersonFirstNameProperty).takeRetainedValue() as String
    nameLabel.text = contactName

    if ABPersonHasImageData(person) {
        photo.image = UIImage(data:
ABPersonCopyImageData(person).takeRetainedValue() as NSData)
    }
    dismissViewControllerAnimated(true, completion: nil)
```

}

The above delegate method, peoplePickerNavigationController(didSelectPerson:) is called when user selects a contact from the address book.

Explanation of Code

var contactName = ABRecordCopyValue(person, kABPersonFirstNameProperty).takeRetainedValue() as String

The above code gets the first name of the selected contact and typecast that as a string value which is then assigned to the variable *contactName*.

nameLabel.text = contactName

This sets the *text* property of *nameLabel* to the value assigned to *contactName* variable.

if ABPersonHasImageData(person) {
    photo.image = UIImage(data:
ABPersonCopyImageData(person).takeRetainedValue() as NSData)
  }

Not all contact of your address book has an image. So we first check whether the selected contact has an image. If that is true, we grab that image and set it to the *image* property of *photo* image view.

dismissViewControllerAnimated(true, completion: nil)

Finally, we dismiss the contact picker view controller.

Running the App

If you run the app and click on the button, you will now be able to select a contact to display. Congratulations! You have learned how to access the address book of your iOS device to retrieve information of a contact.

Chapter 14 - Using the Accelerometer

iPhone and iPads have the Accelerometer built in it. The Accelerometer detects the movement and tilting of the device. In this section, we will show to detect the tilt and movement of a device.

Getting Started

Create a new Single View iPhone application and name it as *Direction*.

Singe click Main.storyboard file and drag a new label into the view.

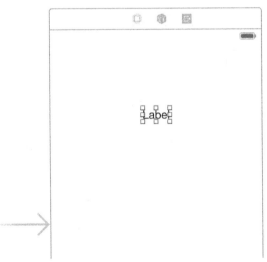

Figure: Add label to storyboard

Open the *ViewController.swift* file and add an outlet for the label -

@IBOutlet weak var orientation: UILabel!

Connect the outlet with label.

Now, add the following code in bold to *ViewController.swift* file -

import UIKit
import CoreMotion

```
class ViewController: UIViewController {

    @IBOutlet weak var orientation: UILabel!
    var motionManager = CMMotionManager()

    override func viewDidLoad() {
    super.viewDidLoad()

    if motionManager.accelerometerAvailable {
    let queue = NSOperationQueue()

    motionManager.startAccelerometerUpdatesToQueue(queue, withHandler: {(data:
CMAccelerometerData!, error: NSError!) in

                if data.acceleration.x > 0.5 {
                self.orientation.text = "Right side"
                } else if data.acceleration.x < -0.5 {
                self.orientation.text = "Left side"
                } else if data.acceleration.y > 0.5 {
                self.orientation.text = "Upside down"
                } else if data.acceleration.y < -0.5 {
                self.orientation.text = "Standing up"
                } else if data.acceleration.z > 0.5 {
                self.orientation.text = "Face down"
                } else if data.acceleration.z < -0.5 {
                self.orientation.text = "Face up"
                }
            })
        }
        }
}
```

In the above code, we import CoreMotion framework and use *CMMotionManager* to detect tilt of the device.

Running the App

Deploy the project to a device and notice that the message on the label changes to the orientation of the device.

Explanation

import CoreMotion

In order to use the accelerometer functionality, we need to import the *CoreMotion* framework.

```
var motionManager = CMMotionManager()
```

The *CMMotionManager* is the gateway to the motion services provided by the iOS framework. Since we work with the accelerometer of the device, we create an instance of *CMMotionManager* and assign that to the variable named **motionManager**.

```
if motionManager.accelerometerAvailable {
```

Before we run any accelerometer specific code, we make sure the accelerometer feature is available on the device. If that's the case, we run the following code -

```
let queue = NSOperationQueue()

motionManager.startAccelerometerUpdatesToQueue(queue, withHandler:
    {(data: CMAccelerometerData!, error: NSError!) in

    if data.acceleration.x > 0.5 {
        self.orientation.text = "Right side"
    } else if data.acceleration.x < -0.5 {
        self.orientation.text = "Left side"
    } else if data.acceleration.y > 0.5 {
        self.orientation.text = "Upside down"
    } else if data.acceleration.y < -0.5 {
        self.orientation.text = "Standing up"
    } else if data.acceleration.z > 0.5 {
        self.orientation.text = "Face down"
    } else if data.acceleration.z < -0.5 {
        self.orientation.text = "Face up"
    }
})
```

The *startAccelerometerUpdatesToQueue(withHandler:)* instance method of *CMMotionManager* delivers accelerometer updates on an operation queue (which is of type *NSOperationQueue*). To understand how it works, you need to be familiar with Grand Central Dispatch (GCD), which is unfortunately an advanced topic and out of the scope of this book.

What you need to know is, when there is any accelerometer update, the if-else-if code block above which simply updates the label based on accelerometer data will run.

To understand the above if-else-if conditions, have a look at the following figure -

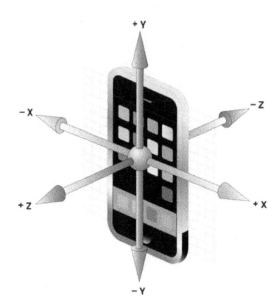

When a tilt is detected, based on the x,y,z coordinates, we select the appropriate message to be displayed in the label.

Device Movement

We have sensed the tilting of the device. But what about the movement of it?

We will extend our application by changing the text of the label when the device is suddenly moved in a particular direction.

Update the *viewDidLoad()* method of *ViewController.swift* with the following code -

```
override func viewDidLoad() {
  super.viewDidLoad()

  if motionManager.accelerometerAvailable {
    let queue = NSOperationQueue()

    motionManager.startAccelerometerUpdatesToQueue(queue, withHandler: {(data:
CMAccelerometerData!, error: NSError!) in

        if data.acceleration.x > 1.3 {
          self.orientation.text = "Right"
        } else if data.acceleration.x < -1.3 {
          self.orientation.text = "Left"
        } else if data.acceleration.y > 1.3 {
          self.orientation.text = "Forward"
        } else if data.acceleration.y < -1.3 {
          self.orientation.text = "Backward"
        } else if data.acceleration.z > 1.3 {
```

```
            self.orientation.text = "Up"
        } else if data.acceleration.z < -1.3 {
            self.orientation.text = "Down"
        }
    })
  }
}
```

Explanation

We increase the magnitude of measurement from 0.5 to 1.3 such that only a movement large enough can trigger a change of text in the label. Upon detecting a such movement in any particular direction, we change the text of the label to that direction.

Running the App

Deploy and run the project on your device. Notice that the text changes when you move the device. If the change is not sensitive enough, you might want to decrease the value from 1.3.

Appendix A - Deploying your App to a Device

Other than testing your apps on the simulator, it is important to know how to deploy them on an actual device. Features such as the accelerometer, camera etc can only be tested on an actual device.

First, you need to sign up for the paid iOS developer program which costs $99 per year. You can do so at: https://developer.apple.com/programs/ios/.

iOS Developer Program

The fastest path from code to customer.

Enroll now $99/year

Figure: Enroll to iOS developer program

Before you can run your app on iOS devices, you need to digitally sign it with something called a *Development Certificate*. If you want to submit apps to the *App Store*, you must sign them with another certificate, the *Distribution Certificate*. You also need to create a *Provisioning Profile*, which is used by Xcode to sign the app for use on your device.

Any iOS device you want to use with Xcode must be registered with your *Developer Program* account. In the following sections, we will walk through the steps on how to do this.

Connecting Your iOS Device

Unlike previous versions, with Xcode 6, creating certificates and provisioning profiles isn't as difficult. First, connect your iOS device (iPhone, iPod touch or iPad, any of these will work) to your Mac using the USB cable. From the Xcode menu, navigate to **Window** → **Devices**, which will open Xcode's *Devices* window -

Figure: Connect iOS device to your Mac using USB cable

On the left, you can see a list of devices used for development. From this list select your device. If its the first time you are using that device with Xcode, you will see a message similar to "*YourName*'s iPhone is not paired with your computer." Unlock the device (slide to unlock) and an alert will pop up on your device asking you to trust the computer you are trying to pair with. Click **Trust** to continue.

The device page of Xcode will be refreshed and you will be able to use your device for development. If you get any error, unplug the device and reboot it. Also make sure you restart Xcode before you reconnect the device.

Setting Up a Developer Program Account with Xcode

In this section, we assume you have already registered and paid for the iOS Developer program. Otherwise do that before you continue the following steps.

From Xcode's menu bar, select **Xcode** → **Preferences** → **Accounts**.

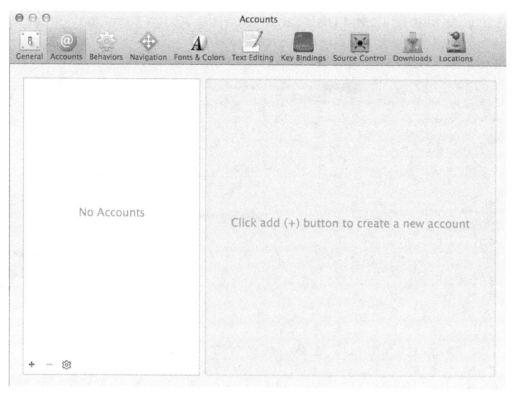

Figure: Accounts tab

Next, add your Apple ID. Click the **+** button at the bottom left corner of accounts tab and choose **Add Apple ID**.

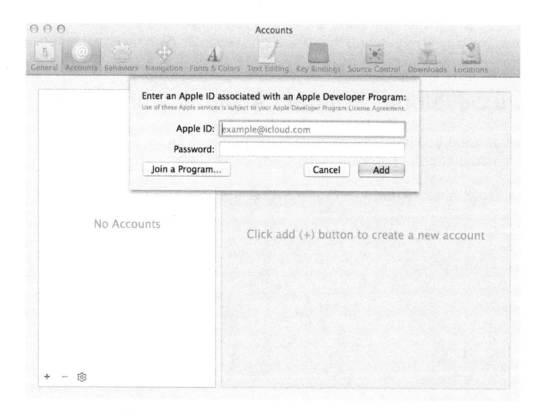

Enter your username and password for your iOS developer program. If you have correctly entered your credentials, Xcode will add your account to the accounts window. After you successfully added your account, click the **View Details...** button located at the bottom-right corner of the accounts window. This will bring up another panel -

Figure: Signing identities and provisioning profiles

This panel lists your signing identities (certificates) and provisioning profiles. This panel is currently empty. You need to click the little arrow in the bottom-left corner and Xcode will try to contact the iOS Dev Center to fetch any certificates and provisioning profiles that you already have. But since you haven't created any of those yet, you should get the following message -

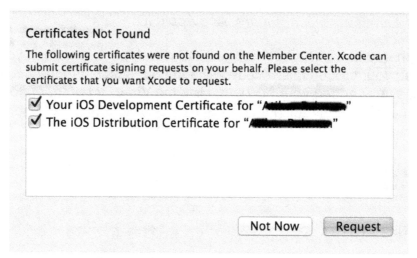

Figure: Certificate signing request

In order to deploy the app to your device, you only need a development certificate. You will later need a distribution certificate for distributing your app in the App store. So, select both options and click **Request**.

Within a few moments, Xcode will automatically register your device with your Developer Program account, create two new certificates (development certificate and distribution certificate) and download and install a Team Provisioning Profile on your device.

Now close the accounts window and return to the Devices window. Right click on your device name from the left panel and select **Show Provisioning Profiles**. This will bring a window that shows all the provisioning profiles installed on that device -

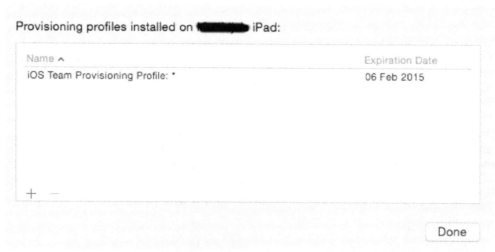

Figure: Provisioning profiles installed on your device

The Team Provisioning Profile has a wildcard *App ID* (*) which means that this provisioning profile can be used for any application you develop (if the application

140

doesn't require special features). That takes care of the setup steps. You are ready to run your app on your device!

Though its not necessary you can also login to your iOS Dev Center website to check your provisioning profiles and other stuffs at:

https://developer.apple.com/devcenter/ios/index.action

Deploying an App on to your Device

To start deploying your app to a device, select the connected device beside the **Run** button.

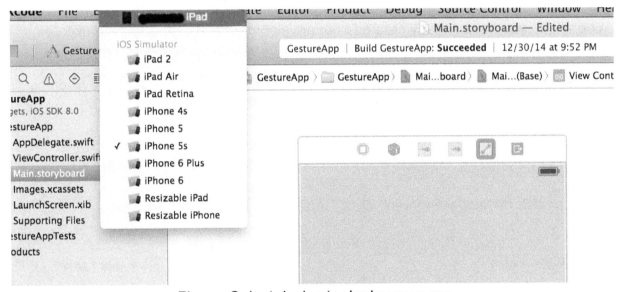

Figure: Select device to deploy your app

Click the **Run** button to launch the app. You should get a popup with the question "codesign wants to sign using key... in your keychain". If you get such a popup, select **Always Allow**. Now you should see your app running on your own device!

If something goes wrong, make sure you check the above steps carefully and try again. If you need further help, you can check the official apple documentation -

https://developer.apple.com/library/mac/documentation/IDEs/Conceptual/
AppDistributionGuide/LaunchingYourApponDevices/LaunchingYourApponDevices.html

Appendix B - Submitting to the App Store

To prepare submitting your app to the App Store, you need to use a distribution certificate instead of a development certificate.If you had gone through the steps in Appendix A, you have already created both development and distribution certificates when you deployed your app to a device.

Instead of a development provisioning profile, you will need a distribution provisioning profile. We will go through how to do that from iOS dev center.

Login to the iOS dev center with your Apple ID -

https://developer.apple.com/ios/

Under the iOS developer Program, click 'Certificates, Identifiers & Profiles' -

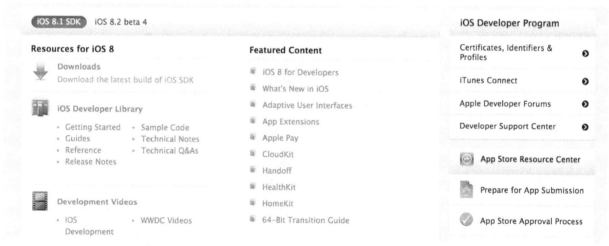

Figure: Select Certificates, Identifiers & Profiles

From the next page, under the iOS Apps section, select Provisioning Profiles -

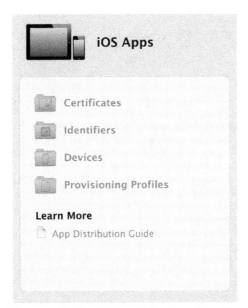

Figure: Select Provisioning Profiles

Click the **+** button to create a new provisioning profile -

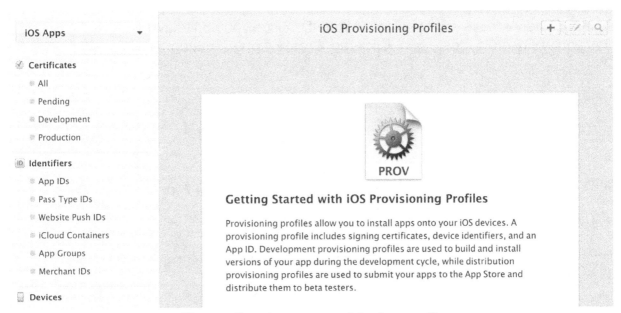

Figure: Create new provisioning profile

You need to select the type of provisioning profile you are going to create. Under the distribution section, select **App Store**.

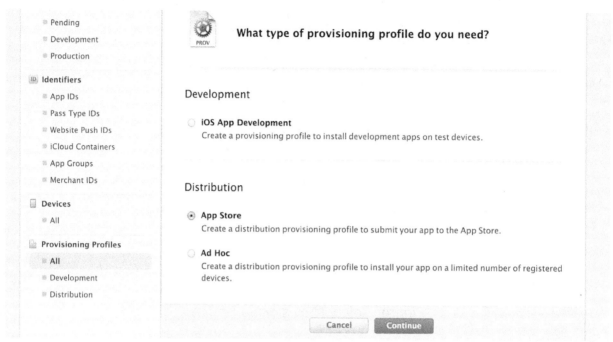

Figure: Select App Store for new provisioning profile

The next step will ask you to select an App ID. Since you don't have an App ID created yet, you will need to create one. Click the '**Create App ID**' button.

Figure: Select App ID for provisioning profile

App IDs are used to identify applications. Enter a description for the App ID. It can be anything!

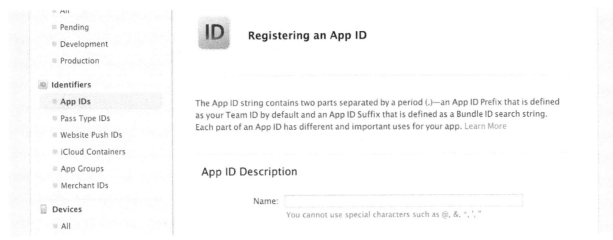

Figure: Enter App ID description

The *App ID Prefix* field will be automatically generated for you.

For *App ID Suffix* field, select **Wildcard App ID** and enter the value as

com.yourdomainname.*

(Replace com.yourdomainname with your own domain in reverse domain notation. This should match the organization identifier you used while creating your app.).

The asterisk (*) at the end of the above value signifies that this single App ID can be used for all your apps.

You could also have selected an *Explicit App ID.* In that case, you have to create an individual App ID for each app submitted to the App Store, like -

com.yourdomainname.appname1
com.yourdomainname.appname2
...

If your app uses any special feature (like iCould), then you will have to create an *Explicit App ID*.

Click the *Continue* button and then complete the App ID creation process.

Now, back to the provisioning profile creation process. From the left panel, select **Provisioning Profiles** → **Distribution** and then click the **+** button. From the next screen, select type of the provisioning profile as **App Store** (under the distribution section) and click continue. (these are the same steps you followed in the App ID creation process). Now, the next screen allows you to select an App ID.

Figure: Select App ID for provisioning profile

Select the App ID you created earlier and click continue. In the next step, you will select the certificate.

Figure: Select certificate

You should see the distribution certificate your created from Xcode (in 'Deploying app to your device' chapter). Select the iOS distribution certificate and click continue.

The next step will let you generate the provisioning profile.

Figure: Generate provisioning profile

Give a profile name and click **Generate.** At this stage, your provisioning profile will be ready for download.

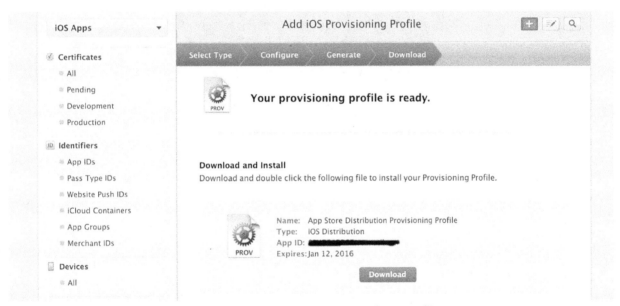

Figure: Download provisioning profile

Download the provisioning profile and double click the downloaded file to install it.

From Xcode, go to the **Preferences → Accounts → View Details** and you will see that, the provisioning profile will be shown there -

Figure: Provisioning profile

Now you have the distribution provisioning profile set up.

From the project navigator, click the project name and go to '**Build Settings**'.

Under the **Code Signing → Code Signing Identity → Release → Any iOS SDK**, select **iOS Distribution**.

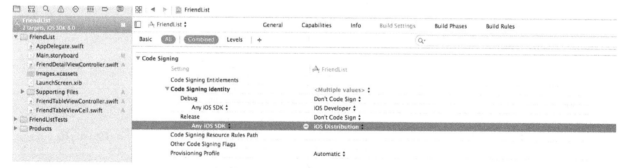

Figure: Set code signing identity

Now from the Xcode toolbar device selection dropdown, select iOS Device (or if your device is connected, select device name). Next, from the dropdown menu located left to the device selection dropdown, select '**Edit Scheme...**' -

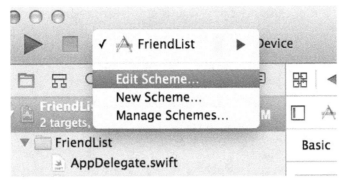

Figure: Select Edit Scheme...

From the next screen, select **Archive** from the left panel and choose *Build Configuration* as '**Release**' and ensure the '**Reveal Archive in Organizer**' checkbox is checked.

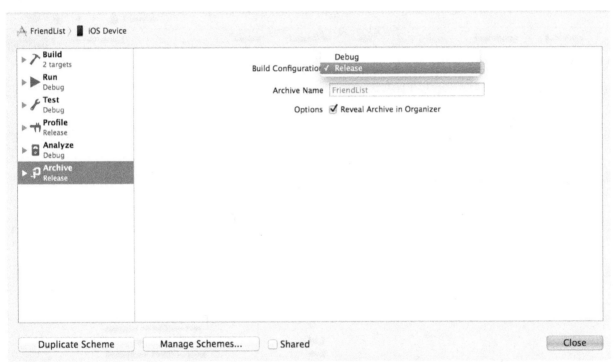

Figure: Select Build Configuration

Click the '**Close**' button.

To submit to the App Store, click on **Product** → **Archive**.

Figure: Archive the project

Your app should appear in the **Archives** section of the Organizer.

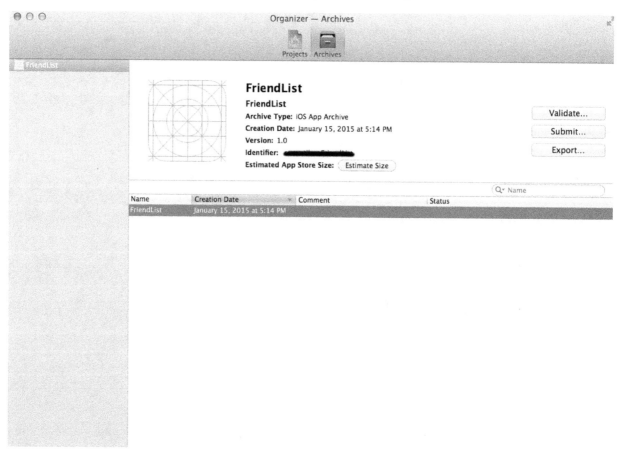

Figure: App shown in Archives

You can proceed to 'Validate' and 'Submit' your app to App Store.

Further details about submitting your app to the App store (eg. icons) are beyond the scope of this book. They are however readily available at developer.apple.com. They contain comprehensive information on submission.

Author's Note

Hello and thank you for reading our book. We would love to get your feedback, learning what you liked and didn't for us to improve. Please feel free to email us at support@i-ducate.com

If you didn't like the book, please email us and let us know how we could improve it. This book can only get better thanks to readers like you.

If you like the book, I would appreciate if you could leave us a review too.

Thank you and all the best to your learning journey in iOS application development.